Advance Praise for
Managing Up

"*Managing Up* offers a new lens through which to view workplace relationships, turning potential conflicts into opportunities for growth. With real-world examples and clear frameworks, this book helps you decode your boss's behavior and unlock the career success you deserve."

—**Daniel H. Pink, #1** *New York Times* **bestselling author of** *Drive,*
To Sell Is Human, **and** *The Power of Regret*

"Wilding has accomplished something rare and invaluable, which is combining bigger-picture insight with specific advice so that readers walk away with concrete, practical advice to experiment with. I am already thinking about how to use the insights with my own colleagues and board members, even as I buy copies for my own direct reports to help them deal with me."

—**Sheila Heen, coauthor of** *Difficult Conversations*
and faculty at Harvard Law School

"Outstanding. Wilding's scripts and strategies show us a better way to get ahead at work."

—**Greg McKeown,** *New York Times* **bestselling author**
of *Essentialism* **and** *Effortless*

"Finally, a science-based book that reveals how to influence others regardless of where you sit on the org chart. It's a resource you'll return to again and again!"

—**Dr. Tasha Eurich,** *New York Times* **bestselling author**
of *Shatterproof, Insight,* **and** *Bankable Leadership*

"A masterclass in the most critical soft skill for career success. Wilding delivers a refreshingly modern, easy-to-follow instruction manual for navigating workplace dynamics with integrity and emotional intelligence."

—**Dorie Clark,** *Wall Street Journal* **bestselling author of** *The Long Game* **and executive education faculty at Columbia Business School**

"If you ever find yourself struggling to figure out where you stand in the workplace, you need this book. Packed with relatable stories and practical scripts and strategies, *Managing Up* is an essential guide for learning how to take back your power and advocate for yourself with confidence."

—**Liz Fosslien,** *Wall Street Journal* **bestselling coauthor of** *No Hard Feelings* **and** *Big Feelings*

"*Managing Up* is not just a book about navigating relationships in the workplace, though it certainly is that—it's a call to arms to reclaim autonomy in your career."

—**Simone Stolzoff, author of** *The Good Enough Job*

"Expertly managing up is an essential skill that everyone needs to learn. Whether you are at the start of your career or have just stepped into a leadership position, Wilding is the perfect mentor for teaching you how to leverage your manager."

—**Vanessa Van Edwards, founder of Science of People and bestselling author**

"Wilding masterfully explains how to thoughtfully navigate those difficult conversations that often define our career trajectory and turn what can be an anxiety-ridden, transactional relationship with our boss into a true partnership."

—**Amy Gallo, cohost of HBR's** *Women at Work* **podcast and author of** *Getting Along*

Managing
Up

Managing
Up

How to Get What You Need
from the People in Charge

Melody Wilding, LMSW

**CROWN
CURRENCY**

CROWN CURRENCY
An imprint of the Crown Publishing Group
A division of Penguin Random House LLC
currencybooks.com

Library of Congress Cataloging-in-Publication Data
Names: Wilding, Melody J., author. Title: Managing up : how to get what you need from the people in charge / by Melody Wilding, LMSW.
Identifiers: LCCN 2024036596 (print) | LCCN 2024036597 (ebook) |
ISBN 9780593444658 (hardcover) | ISBN 9780593444665 (ebook)
Subjects: LCSH: Communication in personnel management. |
Communication in organizations. | Interpersonal communication.
Classification: LCC HF5549.5.C6 W525 2025 (print) |
LCC HF5549.5.C6 (ebook) | DDC 658.4/5—dc23/eng/20240918
LC record available at https://lccn.loc.gov/2024036596
LC ebook record available at https://lccn.loc.gov/2024036597

Hardcover ISBN 978-0-593-44465-8
Ebook ISBN 978-0-593-44466-5

Editor: Leah Trouwborst and Paul Whitlatch
Editorial assistants: Cierra Hinckson and Amy Li
Production editor: Natalie Blachere
Text designer: Amani Shakrah
Production manager: Jessica Heim
Copy editor: Maureen Clark
Proofreaders: Rob Sternitzky and Ann Roberts
Publicist: Josie McRoberts
Marketer: Rachel Rodriguez

Illustrations © Shutterstock (thought bubbles: MayProject; sticky notes: berkah jaya material; business woman, page 252, left: Alphavector; business woman, page 252, right: Drawlab19)

Manufactured in the United States of America

9 8 7 6 5 4 3 2 1

First Edition

To Brian, who manages to fill every day
of our life together with joy and love

CONTENTS

Laura was used to getting tough feedback, but nothing in her career had prepared her for the mixed messages and moving goalposts she faced in her role as head of communications. Weeks earlier, her boss—the CEO—had praised her work overhauling the company's website. But then, just the day before, he had sat Laura down and told her, "I'm not sure if you're in over your head, incompetent, or both."

Laura had joined the startup two and a half years earlier, transitioning from director of public affairs for a large university to the faster-paced and less bureaucratic tech world. At first, she flourished as product communications manager, writing compelling white papers, implementing a dashboard to track campaign metrics, and even jumping in to field press inquiries after a major software crash affected thousands of customers. Her drive, scrappiness, and ability to motivate her team of five direct reports stood out, and within eighteen months she had been tapped to head communications for the entire company.

Laura enthusiastically stepped into her leadership role, eager to prove herself to her new boss and peers right away. Sensing that the CEO was swamped raising venture capital and not wanting to "bother him," Laura took it upon herself to redo the company's online messaging and positioning. In her product role, she had observed that average customers were turned off by technical jargon, so she decided that the company's website and all of their materials would benefit from more user-friendly language.

In spite of all her hard work and the appreciation of her peers, Laura was still adrift when it came to her boss. One day, he'd tell her the new copy she had put together was so impressive that they'd featured it in an investor pitch deck. The next, he'd question why she was wasting time on "low value" tasks instead of focusing on strategy. When Laura pinged him on Slack with questions, he'd ignore her for days, then suddenly respond with a barrage of requests. Laura felt like she couldn't get a clear read on what her boss really wanted . . . and might never be able to figure it out.

She was losing confidence in herself. Once a top performer, she now found herself totally clueless about what was required to succeed at this new level. She was putting in long hours, striving to make big changes and prove her value, yet it seemed like her moves weren't well received by the person who mattered most in her career: her boss. As she watched other senior leaders navigate their roles with apparent ease, she couldn't help but feel inadequate—and *really* annoyed.

Laura's not the only one. During the last few years, the number of professionals who believe they have little to no control over their careers, futures, and work relationships has doubled. A staggering 40 percent of workers grapple with a sense of helplessness. And for more than a decade, as an executive coach to professionals and leaders at some of the world's top companies, I've witnessed countless clients struggle to figure out where they stand in the workplace, a challenge that's become even more urgent and pronounced since the pandemic. These smart, successful people end up constantly questioning whether to share their thoughts or stay silent and blame themselves for missing out on opportunities because they're "not good enough." Others feel boxed in by office politics, frustrated by a lack of change, sidelined by an ambiguous decision-making process, or exhausted by miscommunication and butting heads with colleagues. Though their difficulties seem distinct at first—from "How do I get my ideas taken seriously by upper management?" and "How can I disagree with my boss without jeopardizing my job?" to "Why do I always get overlooked for opportunities despite my hard work?"—their problems often boil down to one thing: **They don't know how to manage up.**

I define "managing up" as strategically navigating relationships with those who have more positional power than you, namely your boss. It's a critical skill set for maneuvering through the complex web of power dynamics, conversations, and unspoken expectations that shape our daily work lives. The idea of managing up has been around for decades, but in a search for greater insight and innovative tools I could use in my own practice, I surveyed a diverse group of twelve thousand people and held interviews with dozens of future readers (if you were one of them, thank you!). From the moment the results started to come back, it was clear that most professionals know they *need* to manage up, but few know *how* to do it well. They understand that in today's workplace, it's no longer necessary to bow to their boss's every wish, but they don't know how to achieve a sense of freedom and control at work without stepping on toes.

You probably picked up this book because you can relate. Even if you have a steady paycheck, a nice title, or other external markers of success, you want *more*. Maybe you're searching for greater peace and ease in your interactions at work so you can get things done with fewer barriers and less stress. Perhaps you want a bigger say in how, when, and where you do your job and to have greater influence on the direction your career takes. Whatever it is, we're going to turn what currently seems impossible into your new reality.

In the old days, managing up equated to making the boss happy, no matter what. That meant keeping your head down, sticking to your job description, and following orders without a peep of disagreement. And let's not forget sucking up. Talk about a recipe for feeling undervalued and stuck! It's not your job, as some books and articles will tell you, to charm and flatter your boss into treating you well, read their mind when they aren't communicating clearly, or work double time to compensate for their incompetence. Some managers truly are too difficult or disorganized to have a healthy relationship with. But most of the stress and frustration that people experience with their bosses is fixable, stemming not from pure incompetence or antagonism but from a lack of awareness on both sides about how to work together effectively.

This book offers a modern, assertive approach to managing up. It's about learning how to get your needs met, whether you want approval to hire a freelancer to help finish a big project on time, the flexibility to work from another city, or the safety of an office environment where you're not afraid to speak your mind.

I've spent the past decade wearing many hats—therapist, human behavior researcher, executive coach. And in that time, I've helped thousands of professionals—from early-career managers to senior leaders at Fortune 500 companies—learn to navigate workplace dynamics and advocate for themselves with confidence. This book will show you exactly how to apply the principles of emotional intelligence, influence, persuasion, negotiation, and more to give yourself a competitive edge at work. After all, without understanding psychology, the workplace—and the people within it—can seem mysterious and infuriating. But once you know what makes your boss tick, you'll be able to work with them so smoothly it'll feel like cheating.

The first step is to adopt a strategic, investigative mindset. When you start to see your boss not just as a gatekeeper or an overseer but as a human being who's contending with their own pressures, distractions, and demands from higher-ups, you'll start to uncover what drives their decisions and unlock how best to communicate with them. That knowledge is key to advocating for what you need. When you can identify the fears and motivations that drive upper management's decisions, you can present your ideas and opinions to get a yes. And cracking the code on your organization's unspoken rules and norms means you can pick the perfect time to ask for more money or a promotion. Want the exact words to say in a tough negotiation or the perfect response to use when you need to push back on a project? I've got you covered. You'll see how to apply surprising, research-based strategies in ways you never thought possible, turning every managing-up moment into one that grows your confidence and advances your career.

You might be wondering, "Why is managing up *my* responsibility? Shouldn't my manager just be better at their job?" It's a fair point—leaders definitely need to pull their weight, and organizations must make sure workplaces are good for our mental health. But here's the deal: **Managing up isn't really about making your boss's life easier. It's about taking control of your own work experience.** Think of it this way: Even if you have a good relationship with those above you, why settle for *good* when it could be *great*? Instead of seeing this process as "extra effort" or "invisible labor," consider it an investment in your satisfaction at work. Don't ask, "Why should I have to manage up?" The real question is "Why wouldn't I want to seize every opportunity to make my career better?"

The Ten Conversations

So how do you move from seeing yourself as a victim of workplace whims to someone who has the power to shape their entire work experience into one that's more fulfilling, easeful, and on their own terms? Introducing the ten conversations.

Each of the chapters ahead tackles one key "conversation" you may need to have with your manager. These aren't one-time chats but rather ongoing conversations that you'll revisit and which will evolve. Some are structured, like your weekly one-on-one with your boss or your annual performance review. Others are more informal, like a quick hallway chat with a colleague or a pre-meeting catch-up with a senior leader. But all of them are opportunities to gather valuable information, build trust and credibility, and shape how you're perceived by those around you.

The conversations build on one another, so we'll start with the most foundational and work our way up to the more advanced. Don't worry about memorizing the order—in real life, they'll often overlap and intersect. The key is to see every interaction, no matter how small, as a chance to put these techniques into practice and gradually strengthen your relationships.

Chapter One: The Alignment Conversation. *How do I stop feeling pulled in a hundred different directions? Why am I spending so much energy trying to decipher cryptic feedback or mixed messages from my boss? How do I know which tasks are most crucial to focus on?* I'll show you how to ask the *right* questions—ones that reveal insights about your manager's unspoken needs and priorities without putting them on the defensive. By focusing on promotable work, you can achieve more in less time, freeing up mental space and energy for your life outside the office.

Chapter Two: The Styles Conversation. *Why does my boss chase every idea that pops into her head? How come he's so short with me—does he hate me?* You'll find out how to decode your boss's communication styles and work habits so you can build rapport, quit overthinking interactions, and tailor your messages, presentations, and emails to get the attention they deserve. You'll also discover how to assert your own needs in a way that commands respect and still keeps higher-ups on your side.

Chapter Three: The Ownership Conversation. *How do I get out from under the bureaucracy or constant micromanagement that's holding me back? What can I do to present—and go after—my ideas without overstepping? If I have an idea for fixing an inefficient process or a problem that's driving me crazy, how can I get buy-in from my boss and colleagues?* Ditch the order-taker mentality and tackle the workplace issues and bottlenecks that bother you. I'll teach you how to "read the room" and accurately judge the best moments to advocate for change. You'll walk away knowing how to craft and pitch your proposals in ways that prompt your manager or others to give you the green light to move ahead.

Chapter Four: The Boundaries Conversation. *What do I say when my manager dumps yet another task on my plate? What if they flip out when I say no?* Discover the hidden costs of being "too helpful" and learn to push back with tact and confidence. From navigating sensitive topics to declining tasks in a way that adds to your credibility, this chapter is packed with scripts and strategies for setting boundaries that stick—even with the most demanding bosses and colleagues.

Chapter Five: The Feedback Conversation. *Should I risk saying something to my boss about an issue that's upsetting me, or should I just let it go? What do I do when it seems like my feedback to them went in one ear and out the other?* This chapter will guide you to carefully and constructively confront your manager about everything from their lack of vision to their favoritism of another colleague. I'll give you scripts and frameworks to get your voice taken seriously and specific-yet-subtle strategies to make sure your input is acted upon.

Chapter Six: The Networking Conversation. *How do I determine who, besides my boss, I should be spending time with? How do I ask for a favor or support without it feeling awkward?* We begin this chapter by identifying where key decision-makers typically spend their time and how you can naturally intersect with these spaces. You'll then learn exactly how to get influential people to say yes to meeting with you, and more important, how to ask for help in a way that feels organic and strengthens your social capital over the long term.

Chapter Seven: The Visibility Conversation. *Why does my hard work continue to go unnoticed? How do I share my accomplishments without sounding like a conceited a-hole?* Right now you may be missing out on everyday chances to elevate your reputation and attract exciting opportunities. You'll change that through the science of storytelling and presenting your skills and results in a memorable, authoritative way. We'll also cover how to handle credit-stealing colleagues and a manager who excludes you.

Chapter Eight: The Advancement Conversation. *How do I position my-self for a promotion, bigger projects, or a move to a different team? What if my manager blocks my progress?* Even though no one cares about your aspirations more than you do, the reality is that the best way to get ahead is by aligning with what your manager wants and the organization needs. I'll show you how to make that connection, get your boss's buy-in on your plans, and navigate objections that arise along the way about your readiness, the timing, and more.

Chapter Nine: The Money Conversation. *How do I make a compelling case for better compensation? What if a higher salary isn't possible right now?* Negotiating is more than just throwing out a number; it involves a tricky dance of invisible incentives and underlying tensions. That's why in this chapter you'll find out how to gauge your worth and justify it convincingly. And don't worry if more money is off the table. You'll be armed with creative ways to get other perks that can be equally valuable.

Chapter Ten: The Quitting Conversation. *How do I know when it's time to move on? What can I do to exit on good terms?* Sometimes the best way to get ahead is to switch jobs or companies altogether. How you leave is how you'll be remembered, so I'll also walk you through everything you need to do to transition out smoothly, how to handle those awkward "I'm quitting" moments, and ways to keep your reputation and relationships glowing, even if you and your boss don't end on the best terms.

The scripts and strategies you'll encounter will work regardless of your industry and company size—whether you're new to your job and want to start off on the right foot or you've been in your role for years and need to reteach people how to treat you. While it's fun to mock corporate speak and workplace jargon, knowing how to craft your words in this context is key to being taken seriously. So I'll show you how to adjust your language for each conversation— when to keep it light and when to dial up the formality, how to balance sincerity with professionalism and realness with reserve. It's no secret that some workplaces and relationships are rife with bias, so we'll also tackle situations when you face inequality, prejudice, and discrimination. Throughout the book you'll hear real stories from my clients as well as insights from thousands of readers I surveyed, including through quotes at the beginning of each chapter.

You can download key takeaways, scripts, and templates from each chapter at managingup.com/bonuses.

Take Back Your Power

While I recommend following the conversations in order, feel free to jump around based on what feels most relevant to you right now. It's totally fine if you don't put every single strategy into practice right away, but if you take what you need and start making small changes today, they'll add up. As I've witnessed my clients apply what you'll learn in this book, I've seen them accomplish amazing things—earning skip-level promotions, leading million-dollar expansion projects, and receiving awards as top performers in their companies. But what's even more life-changing is how they reclaim a sense of agency, autonomy, and authority in their careers.

That's exactly what happened to Laura, whose story you heard earlier. Through the alignment conversation with the CEO and other senior leaders (chapter 1), she was able to ramp up her company's business-to-business messaging, including creating an enterprise demo process that helped them sell new licenses more quickly. When she got to the bottom of her boss's communication habits through the styles conversation (chapter 2), she stopped taking his brief replies personally and started getting the input she wanted by presenting findings to him in bullet points and texting while he was out courting new investors. The ownership conversation (chapter 3) helped Laura step forward with her ideas and take the reins on projects in a way others rallied behind (instead of railing against). While she still hit some rocky patches along the way, Laura's transformation was so significant that she soon became the CEO's right hand and closest advisor. A few months later, she sent me an excited email saying she was getting a hefty six-figure bonus thanks to the tangible impact she'd made to the bottom line. But even more important, she added, "the sense of assuredness I have now is priceless."

That's because, most of all, everything you'll learn in this book is going to fundamentally change the relationship you have with *yourself*. No matter what life throws at you, you'll move from a "Why does this always happen to me?" mindset to an "I've got this" attitude. So, yes, it's going to take dedication. Yes, it'll take time. But ask yourself, "Am I prepared to turn 'the way things are' into 'the way I want them to be'?" If so, then you're in the right place. Let's go.

CHAPTER ONE

The Alignment Conversation

Stop spinning your wheels and work on what really matters

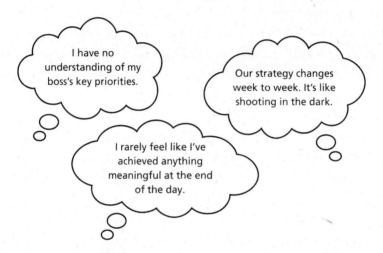

I sensed something was terribly wrong when I dialed into the conference line at 8:00 A.M. and heard an unfamiliar voice. "Hi, Melody, I'm Janine. I'm with an external HR firm. Unfortunately, this call is to let you know that your employment has been terminated, effective immediately." Shock rippled through my body as my boss, who was also on the line, whispered, "I'm so sorry."

On the surface, being laid off came out of the blue. I was working in healthcare while building my coaching practice on the side. During my two years at the company, I had received positive performance reviews and was often praised for my good work. But as

I picked up the pieces after being let go, I saw the situation more clearly. I had been hired to work on a pet project of my manager's, an innovation initiative that was outside the company's core offering. The project, while interesting, lacked buy-in from the senior leadership team and was seen as a money pit.

I was also on an island, both literally and figuratively. I worked remotely from my Manhattan apartment while the rest of the team was headquartered in Boston. Working from home—which was uncommon back then—had presented some barriers, but the real problem was that I hadn't been talking to and listening to others. If I had been, I would have quickly uncovered that my job was out of sync with the company's goals. When the time for cuts came, my role was dispensable, and I had few—if any—advocates willing to fight to keep me or have me assigned to their teams.

For years, I've kept the fact that I was laid off a secret. Competent professionals aren't *let go,* I thought, every time my mind brushed up against the unfortunate start to my life's work. What would it say about me if my colleagues and clients knew my dirty little secret? But now after working with thousands of leaders and executives across the world, I realize that what led to my unceremonious departure wasn't a failure of talent or skill. I had failed to have *the alignment conversation.*

The alignment conversation is all about figuring out how your work fits into the bigger picture and making sure you and your boss agree on what success looks like. Regardless of whether your manager is clear and forthcoming about their goals and priorities, this chapter will help you crack the code on what they *really* want. You'll also discover how to go *beyond* your boss to connect with leaders farther up the chain of command without causing drama. Any discussion of alignment would be incomplete without delving into office politics, so I'll also show you how to map power dynamics and figure out whom you need to stay close to as well as what to do when you're at the whim of ever-changing priorities or dealing with a control freak.

If you've never broached this topic with your boss before, don't panic! Getting fired is an extreme example of what can go wrong when you're not aligned. But you probably will find yourself demoralized and frustrated if there's a yawning gap between your company's goals and what you *think* they are. Because losing your job isn't the only consequence of not having the alignment conversation. You might find yourself left out of important projects, constantly second-guessing your decisions, or continually having to revise and edit your work because it doesn't meet unspoken expectations.

The alignment conversation isn't just the key to deciphering your manager's thought processes and priorities, it's also the best—and maybe the only—way to know for sure you're making a meaningful impact at work. For example, rather than just nodding along during a project kickoff, you can ask, "I noticed that we're starting this around the same time as Y is ramping up. How do these fit together?" to help you piece together your manager's broader strategy and open the door to advocate for resources. Posing a question like "What's the dream scenario for how we handle [tricky situation]?" can reveal information your manager has about stakeholders' concerns, allowing you to fine-tune your approach and avoid land mines.

We're starting with the alignment conversation because it's also the fastest way to make every workday more pleasant—with your boss and beyond. Not only are you laying the groundwork for bigger and better opportunities (plum projects, greater visibility, more money!), you're also saving your sanity. No more stewing about whether you're doing a good job. Instead, you can log on to work each day knowing exactly what's expected of you, sure that you're focusing on the right tasks. No more emotional drain from doing what you *think* your boss expects, only to get it wrong and face frustration and disappointment. By having the alignment conversation, you can replace any simmering tension with a sense of shared purpose and understanding.

Cast Your One-Year Vision

Before you can align with others, you have to know what *you* want. Your one-year vision helps you identify areas where your dreams and aspirations intersect with your team's or company's goals—or uncover where they don't, which we'll deal with later in this chapter and in chapter 8, where we'll discuss turning an okay job into a great one.

So imagine yourself 365 days from now having the best possible workday. What are you doing? Who are you interacting with? What makes this day stand out and feel fulfilling and energized? Use the present tense, as if it's happening now, and describe what you're doing and how you're feeling in vivid detail. Get inspired to create your one-year vision using the following prompts:

- Think about a key relationship that could really improve your job satisfaction. How has this relationship evolved over the past year?

- Imagine you've mastered a new skill or tool that's critical for your career growth. What is this skill or tool, and how did you go about learning it?

- Consider a key project you want to lead. What is it about, who are you working with, and what impact does it have on your team?

- Reflect on any organizational changes that you anticipate in the next year. What does it look like to proactively prepare for this?

- Envision writing a note to a mentor or colleague a year from now. What exciting accomplishments are you sharing?

Here are examples of one-year visions to inspire your own.

Resource Management Specialist

➡ *Today:* All I do is answer urgent emails from park visitors and tour companies. My relationship with my boss is tense because we're always putting out fires. We haven't had the chance to talk about my career growth in more than a year.

➡ *One year from now:* Half of my role is still dedicated to managing logistics, but the other half is focused on educating visitors about the park, which I love. Now, instead of clashing over daily tasks, my manager and I regularly brainstorm ideas together, showing how much our relationship has grown and improved.

Academic Librarian

➡ *Today:* I've thrown myself into curating special collections that highlight different cultures. While students and faculty appreciate my efforts, my initiative seems to be ignored and undervalued by our administration.

➡ *One year from now:* I've been tapped by several professors to integrate our special collections into their curriculums. The dean's chief of staff even invited me to sit on our university's advisory board for undergraduate engagement because of my willingness to go above and beyond.

IT Manager

➡ *Today:* I'm known as the "cloud maestro" because I excel at large-scale tech integrations. But I keep hitting a wall due to a lack of buy-in from higher leadership, leaving promising projects in limbo.

➡ *One year from now:* I'm able to build relationships and a strong coalition with our head of product and head of marketing. They trust me enough to influence our VP to green-light our largest implementation ever, touching ten thousand customers and earning me a promotion.

We'll come back to your one-year vision several times over the course of the book, so you'll get a chance to tweak and refine where you see yourself heading. Even if your goals feel out of reach, don't shut down possibilities just yet. Give yourself permission to dream.

Get in Your Boss's Head

Your boss is busy, and they may not always be forthcoming about what's most important to them, so it's on you to ask the right questions to get what you need. Research from Harvard Business School finds that the simple act of asking a question drastically increases likability and rapport. Choose a few of the questions below to try in an upcoming one-on-one or to weave into conversation. Approach your boss's answers with curiosity. The questions you ask should never feel like an interrogation or take up hours of their time.

To Identify Their Goals and Pressures

- What goals are the most important to you and why are they a priority now?

- What are some of the metrics your own boss discusses with you and how are they calculated?

- What keeps you up at night when thinking about our team or projects?

- What emerging trends should we be mindful of and potentially capitalize on?

To Define What Success Looks Like

- How do my responsibilities and tasks contribute to the overall success of the team/department/organization?

- How am I being measured when it comes to meeting these goals?

- What does good performance look like? Great performance? How can I exceed your expectations when it comes to deliverables and output?

- In terms of impact and value creation, what would you like to see me accomplish in the next three, six, or twelve months and why?

- What assumptions or misconceptions about success in this role do you think should be addressed?

To Clarify Priorities

- What do you wish you had more time to work on and/or what's one thing I could do that would make your job simpler?

- What actions or changes would allow you to look back in ninety days and say, "Wow, that really made a difference"?

- This is how I'm spending my time. Are my priorities consistent with yours? What would you like me to change to support you better?

- We have multiple priorities, so I'd like to understand how X compares to other tasks on my plate. Are there any areas where I should focus more or less?

If it's your first time bringing up the topic of alignment or the relationship with your manager has been rocky, it might feel weird to both of you if the discussion comes out of nowhere. So try one of these scripts: "I'd like to make sure we're on the same page when it comes to our priorities. Chatting about this would help me better understand what's top of mind for you." Or "I've been thinking about how to make sure that what I'm working on supports our overall goals. If I understand your vision and expectations, I can accomplish even more and we can avoid miscommunication."

Dig Deeper

A good question doesn't always lead to a helpful answer. Bosses, like everyone else, can be vague, unclear, or brief in their responses, especially if they're caught off guard, are in a rush, or haven't thoroughly considered the topic before. For example, when Rebecca, a financial advisor, asked the firm's partner about goals for the next quarter, he bluntly said, "Growth is our focus. Period." Even though Rebecca was rattled, she took a deep breath and probed further. "I'd like to have a clearer understanding of how we measure growth so I can work toward the right outcome. What benchmarks would signify progress?" As her boss revealed more, Rebecca continued asking, "And what else?," which gave her the details she needed to move forward. Notice that Rebecca didn't ask why. She saw that her boss was already defensive and asking why could have caused him to feel attacked or as if he had to justify himself, which wouldn't have been great for either of them.

Another strategy I often recommend comes from one of my favorite books, *Never Split the Difference*. Former FBI hostage negotiator and author Chris Voss recommends mirroring or repeating the last few words your counterpart says to encourage them to reveal more detail or depth. For instance, if your boss says, "We need to focus on improving our customer service scores this quarter," you might reply, "Our customer service scores?"

"Yes, it's essential," your boss goes on. "Our recent feedback shows that our customers aren't fully satisfied with our response times."

To which you mirror again, "Not fully satisfied?"

"That's right. We need to be more responsive and solve issues faster."

Bingo! Now you've pinpointed a root cause that you can take ownership of solving (more on that in chapter 3).

Suppose mirroring reveals that your boss is concerned with reducing overhead costs this quarter. Use this insight to prioritize your time, say by negotiating better rates with suppliers. You can also incorporate "cost-cutting" language and data into your reports and presentations, proving that you're attending to their concerns. Mirroring can also help you clarify misunderstandings or highlight achievements that might not be on your boss's radar. For example, if your boss falsely asserts that your team is falling short on targets, you can gently correct the record: "Actually, the latest reports show a 5 percent improvement over last month, though you're right, there are some factors affecting our progress."

Besides problem-solving, you're building rapport by understanding your manager's point beyond the surface level and validating their perspective. Regardless of context, this type of active listening leads to greater relationship satisfaction and a willingness to interact with the listener in the future.

Schedule a Skip-Level

It's not enough to manage up to your boss: One-on-one meetings between you and *your boss's boss* should also be a key part of your plan. Skip-levels not only ensure that the most important person up your chain of command knows who you are and what you're capable of but also give you a more complete picture of the organizational landscape. Before you jump to schedule a meeting with your boss's boss, tread carefully. Some companies encourage open communication, while others may have more hierarchical structures. If you do proceed, transparency is key. Approach your boss, explain your reasoning, and seek their endorsement. Emphasize that your intention is not to undermine or bypass them, but rather to enhance your own understanding and alignment with the organization. Here are a few strategic questions you can ask your manager's manager in these meetings:

- What are the key strategic priorities for our organization in the coming year? How do you see our team supporting these priorities?

- As our organization moves toward its long-term goals, what are some upcoming initiatives or changes we should be aware of?

- In your experience, what are some common challenges or obstacles that teams like ours face in achieving alignment with the organization's goals?

- I'm curious about your vision for our department/team. How do you see us evolving and growing? Are there any particular areas or skills you believe we should focus on to stay ahead in our industry?

- Could you provide some insights into how our team's performance is evaluated at the leadership level? What metrics or indicators do you consider when assessing our success?

It's completely normal to be nervous, but remember that senior leaders *want* to know what's happening on the ground. Pay attention to—and dig deeper into—discrepancies and inconsistencies you hear between what your boss has shared and what your skip-level manager says (e.g., "My understanding is X based on discussions with my manager. Is this right?") and always send a follow-up note to thank your skip-level boss for their time. If you said you would circle back about something, do it! Show that you're reliable and take their time seriously. Also, consider asking for a quarterly meeting and get it on the calendar as soon as possible.

STEAL THESE SCRIPTS

How you ask for what you want at work is often just as important as *what* you ask for. Use the scripts below as is or tailor the tone based on the culture of your organization.

To your manager

As part of my professional growth, I'd like to broaden my perspective about what matters to the company and where we're going. Meeting with [your boss's manager] would allow me to learn more about our organization's goals and then align my work to contribute to our team's objectives. My intention isn't in any way to bypass you. I view this as a chance to complement the guidance and support you provide while also understanding the broader strategic context from [your boss's manager]. Would you be open to that? Your support would mean a lot.

To your manager's manager

Could we meet for thirty minutes in the coming weeks? I have a lot of respect for your expertise and leadership, particularly in [area], and I've enjoyed learning from you from afar. In my role as [your job title], it's important I have a better understanding of our company's priorities, challenges, and opportunities, so I'd love to hear your thoughts on what's ahead as well as any other guidance or recommendations. I can also share my observations and experiences from the team's day-to-day operations. Happy to be flexible and accommodate your availability.

Beyond the Conversation

Get It in Writing

While alignment with your boss is crucial, being in sync with your colleagues helps you get things done from day to day and makes work a lot easier and relaxed. Have you ever come out of a meeting sure of your next steps only to discover days later that your colleagues had a totally different interpretation of how you planned to move forward? While it may seem like creating "share-outs" is just glorified note-taking, these concise meeting recaps will not only give well-functioning teams a way to revisit next steps but also cement your position as the go-to person for information (which is a verified source of power). And if your team *isn't* great at clarity, then you can easily become a leader who either helps guide the group toward a game plan or holds others accountable.

To make the share-out process as easy as possible, create a template that includes sections for key discussion points, agreed-upon actions, and deadlines. Then be open for input from your colleagues so that you're sure to identify misalignment early. You're not writing the next great American novel here—keep it to three to five bullet points per section and move on.

Hi all, to make sure we're on the same page after today's call, see below:

Main Takeaways:
- Discussed the upcoming project launch timeline and identified potential roadblocks.
- Reviewed the Q1 metrics and areas for improvement.
- Explored strategies for increasing customer engagement.

Action Items:
Project Launch Timeline:
- Who: John to coordinate with the marketing team.
- What: Finalize the promotional material.
- When: Complete by March 15.

Performance Improvement:
- Who: Sarah to lead a review of customer feedback.
- What: Identify three areas for immediate action.
- When: Report findings by March 20.

Customer Engagement Strategies:
- Who: Entire team to brainstorm tactics.
- What: Compile a list of actionable ideas.
- When: Schedule implementation session for March 25.

You can also rotate responsibility for this documentation so you're not always saddled with the extra effort, or even outsource it to an AI notetaker app.

Plot Your Power Map

You don't matter to everybody, and everybody shouldn't matter to you. That's why you should always be asking yourself, "*Who* do I need to be aligned with?" when you consider key stakeholders, leaders, groups, or influential figures in the workplace. Of course, if you have a genuine connection with someone, it doesn't matter what they do within the organization, but when it comes to deciphering politics, a power map will help you make smart choices about which relationships you invest in . . . and which you don't.

Grab some stickies and assign people to one of four categories, presented below in descending order of importance. Let's take the example of Svetlana, a coordinator at a fragrance company who has to secure approvals for a new scent.

- **Quadrant 1: high influence, high interest.** For Svetlana, this includes heads of other departments like marketing, R&D, and sales. She engages with them more frequently and thoroughly than with others, regularly seeking their input and opinions, providing detailed weekly or daily reports, and proactively involving them in decisions and brainstorming. Since this group is mission-critical to the project's success, and they have a vested interest in its outcomes, Svetlana is forthcoming about challenges and opportunities so they're aware of successes and setbacks.

- **Quadrant 2: high influence, low interest.** People like the chief legal officer (CLO) or a regulatory body like the Bureau of Consumer Protection fall into this category. While both have a lot of say over company policies and Svetlana's plans, they don't care much about the project specifics. Svetlana compiles concise updates on a monthly or quarterly basis and reaches out when there are critical decisions. By connecting their involvement to their own interests or the organization's goals, she secures support without overwhelming them with excessive information.

- **Quadrant 3: low influence, high interest.** Michael, one of Svetlana's peers, and Rachel, a highly specialized formulation scientist, fall into quadrant 3. While enthusiastic, a junior employee like Michael has limited decision-making power, so Svetlana keeps him in the loop with asynchronous email updates versus time-consuming calls. Similarly, although Rachel has a deep interest in the subject matter of the project, she lacks organizational authority as an individual contributor. Svetlana gives her the opportunity to contribute input via a survey and advocates to have Rachel elevated to an advisory role to earn goodwill and boost her perceived status.

- **Quadrant 4: low influence, low interest.** In Svetlana's case, this includes colleagues who are on leave, external vendors and suppliers, and mid-level members of other teams. She has good personal relationships with this group and even has lunch once a week with a colleague in R&D who happens to live in her neighborhood, but

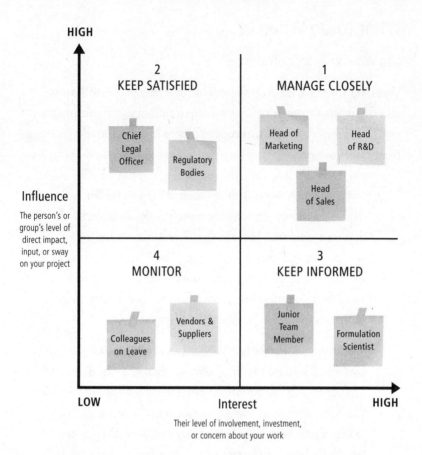

HIGH

2
KEEP SATISFIED

1
MANAGE CLOSELY

Chief Legal Officer

Regulatory Bodies

Head of Marketing

Head of R&D

Head of Sales

Influence

The person's or group's level of direct impact, input, or sway on your project

4
MONITOR

3
KEEP INFORMED

Colleagues on Leave

Vendors & Suppliers

Junior Team Member

Formulation Scientist

LOW

Interest

HIGH

Their level of involvement, investment, or concern about your work

she directs most of her energy to doubling down on quadrants 1 and 2.

A power map is only valuable when it's current, so take time to update it twice a year to account for changes in your colleagues' level of interest or influence. And as circumstances evolve, adjust your strategy accordingly.

What to Do When . . .

You Work with a Control Freak

Working for (or with) someone who scrutinizes everything you do and demands that you run it past them for approval can push anyone to the brink, but don't despair. Here's how to handle an impatient taskmaster:

- **Run with rough drafts.** Rather than toiling away for days—or weeks—to craft the perfect deliverable, do a first pass and say, "Here's what I've put together so far. It's a bit rough around the edges, but I wanted to capture the core ideas and structure so we can shape it into something outstanding." Your boss will be happy to have input, and you'll conserve your energy.

- **Reinforce their authority.** "What we ultimately do is up to you" or "I'll share my two cents so that you can make the final decision" allows you to emphasize you know who's the boss. Pose your ideas as inquiries ("What if . . ." or "How about we . . ."). Asking questions in conversation boosts feelings of control in the other person, which is called the question-behavior effect.

- **Overshare.** Send a breakdown of items you plan to tackle each week every Monday or shoot over a quick heads-up if you'll be late to a meeting. While sometimes tedious, sharing this information will satiate your boss's desire for oversight, while saving you the effort of justifying yourself later: "To keep you in the loop about our progress, I've prepped a weekly status memo with a snapshot of recent developments" or "I'm confirming that we're moving ahead with X. Let me know by Friday if there are any changes."

- **Get ahead of their criticism.** You might say, "I'm planning to approach [task] this way. Do you have initial thoughts?" When your boss corrects you, use the classic "yes, and" improv technique. Acknowledge it ("yes") and then add your perspective or suggestion ("and") to subtly assert your ideas while taking their feedback into account: "Yes, I appreciate the need to be more concise in my emails, and I believe a brief context section is still beneficial for clarity, especially for people less familiar with the project."

- **Ask for the praise you need.** Try emphasizing the significance of their approval: "I enjoy hearing how I can improve. It's also important for me to know what's going well so I can do more of that. Is there room for you to share your perspective on what I'm getting right, or is it your sense that it's not warranted?"

Priorities Conflict or Keep Changing

Do you ever feel like you're playing a never-ending game of Whac-A-Mole? Maybe your boss keeps changing plans, or you're being pulled in different directions by multiple leaders or dueling cross-functional partners. Your entire organization could even be in flux. Whatever the case, here's how to stay the course:

- **Identify reasons for shifting sands.** It's tempting to personalize difficult situations at work when things aren't going your way, but the priority ping-pong probably has nothing to do with you. Is it caused by market changes, a shift in strategic direction, or other factors? It may simply be a lack of focus or fear from above rather than your manager's flightiness or a message to you about the quality of your work.

- **Discern a direction from a passing thought.** You might work for a visionary type who has a hundred new ideas before breakfast. Instead of swinging into action, wait until an idea comes up at least three times before trying to move it forward. Create a "parking lot" to capture their fancies.

- **Slow down the dynamic.** When a colleague or your boss shares a new idea, you can listen and validate without dismissing it: "That's interesting; I'll take a look." Or you can try to gently redirect their attention to agreed-upon plans with a question like "How do you see this new idea fitting in with our current goals?"

- **Identify common ground.** Look for commonalities or shared objectives among the conflicting priorities. Are there overarching goals or principles that everyone agrees on? By identifying areas of alignment, you can focus on finding solutions that satisfy both parties to some extent.

- **Outline the cost.** Instead of assigning blame or getting frustrated, try to renegotiate your understanding of expectations based on new information: "This new task will take twenty hours. Are you comfortable with that?" Inform others of any risks: "If the priority changes, then X will be delayed." After hearing the investment, the person may decide the task can wait or isn't important after all.

You're Totally Misaligned with Your Manager

In extreme cases, your boss's vision and goals may differ drastically from yours—and the organization's as a whole. Maybe they're pursuing a project that conflicts with the company's mission or they're pushing for strategies you believe are completely misguided. In later chapters, we'll talk about disagreeing productively, setting boundaries, and advancing even when your boss throws up roadblocks, but for now, here are a few ways to make the most of the situation:

- **Pick your battles.** Steven, an entry-level account rep, was concerned about his boss's heavy emphasis on cold-calling, so I encouraged him to aim for a 70/30 alignment split—to be aligned 70 percent of the time on the most critical priorities and objectives, and not to stress over the other 30 percent. Since Steven mostly agreed with his boss's decision to prioritize their hottest sales targets, he realized it was okay—even healthy—if he had a different opinion on how to go about it. But I still cautioned him to consider whether pushing back on his boss would lead to a better outcome, or was his objection a matter of personal preference?

- **Bridge the gap.** Steven approached his boss to better understand their divide: "I've noticed we have different views on how to balance short-term sales with long-term client relationships. Could you share your

perspective on this? What are your main priorities?"
He then made a proposal: "What if we dedicate half of
our efforts to relationship-building activities that could
secure future sales alongside cold-calling? We could
experiment with this for two months and then
reevaluate."

- **Show them the light.** By delivering tangible return on
  investment (ROI), you may be able to convince your
  boss something is worthwhile. With his boss's cautious
  approval, Steven organized a series of targeted, intimate
  networking events designed to deepen relationships with
  key prospects. After a few months, Steven's experiment
  began to yield impressive results—higher conversion
  rates and bigger deals, which allowed him to present a
  clearer case for his approach.

- **Identify sympathetic superiors.** Steven started casual chats
  with other managers with observations like "Our team is
  strong on the cold-calling side, but it feels like there's a
  push for permission-based sales in the industry. How do
  you see us fitting into that?" This allowed Steven to
  gather valuable advice and alternative viewpoints
  without appearing to undermine his manager. In
  extreme situations, you might even go directly to senior
  leadership to discuss your ideas and proposals, but going
  over your manager's head is risky, so use this tactic
  sparingly and only once you've established a strong
  relationship with others above you.

- **Explore your options.** Steven's patience paid off and
  eventually his boss came around to doing more

networking events. But not everyone will be that
fortunate. Before you jump ship, ask about a job
rotation or short-term project assignments that
would allow you to work under a different manager
temporarily. Find cross-functional opportunities that
expose you to leaders from other teams. If you explore
a transfer, express your interest in working under
someone else and provide a rationale for the change,
emphasizing how it aligns with the company's needs
and your strengths.

Alignment isn't permanent. For you, your leaders, and everyone
you work with, roles change, priorities change, and life changes, so
having the alignment conversation—in small doses as part of regular check-ins and team meetings and in large ones monthly or
quarterly—will ensure that you're on the same page (most of the
time) with everyone around you, especially with your boss. Take
time this week to cast your one-year vision so you can see more
clearly how your personal goals dovetail with your boss's objectives
and support the work of the entire organization. Think of it as your
road map to intentionally managing up, versus simply blending in
as a yes-person who follows orders without necessarily advancing
your own career or adding concrete value. Make note of one to two
questions from "Get in Your Boss's Head" that you could pose during your next one-on-one. It will eventually become second nature
to weave those insights into both your day-to-day and your long-
range plans, a strength that will make all the difference between
spinning your wheels and reaching the next phase of your career
with your team.

CHAPTER TWO

The Styles Conversation

Work with different personalities without pulling your hair out

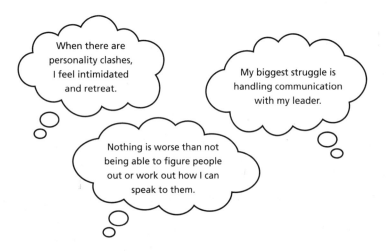

This is the tale of two civil engineers, Adrian and Gabe, who worked for the same boss, Vanessa. They joined their architectural firm as senior project managers at the same time, and although they oversaw different building designs, they were close and relied on each other for support. They even shared the same executive coach—yours truly.

Working with both Adrian and Gabe meant that I came to know Vanessa well. She was an opinionated, hard-charging leader who appreciated quick thinking. Because she had great instincts and design sensibility, this rarely turned out to be a problem for projects, but it did create interpersonal friction with her team. She expected others to keep up with her, to challenge her when necessary, and to put the brakes on if they saw trouble ahead. Neither Gabe nor Adrian had ever worked with someone like her before.

On the one hand, Gabe was often frustrated by how stubborn Vanessa was. "Once she forms a first impression, it's impossible to change her mind." Gabe had been trying to advance one of his team members to manager, which would free up substantial time in his schedule for strategic work. "This person *wasn't* meeting expectations when she joined the team a year ago, but now, with my coaching, she's excelling. Vanessa's fighting me tooth and nail on the promotion, questioning whether she's ready and nitpicking every minor mistake she's made." Gabe felt defeated and internalized Vanessa's constant questioning as evidence of his ineptitude as a leader. "I just don't know anymore if I'm making the right call."

Adrian, on the other hand, approached his relationship with Vanessa like a puzzle. He had come to understand that Vanessa didn't take their back-and-forth personally. Instead she relished his engagement and occasionally even changed her mind when he pushed back. "Even if she says she doesn't want to hear it," he said, "I tell her, 'Give me two minutes to explain the problem and tell you the three things I've tried already before you ask questions and get into solutions. That way we can use your time more effectively.' Other times I have to be even more direct and explain, 'Vanessa, it's important that you're in the loop on this, but I'm not asking for feedback or for you to solve this issue.'" Adrian's willingness to experiment had benefited them both. "Her style can be frustrating," he said, "but when Vanessa wins, we all win."

What Adrian understood that Gabe didn't was that *the styles conversation* is key to understanding how your boss and others approach communication, decision-making, feedback, conflict resolution, and more. If the alignment conversation (chapter 1) helps you get into the heads of those you work with, then the styles conversation is the key to unlocking how you accomplish those things together, which begins by nonjudgmentally unpacking the personalities and psychology of the people you work most closely with. When you can adapt and adjust to different styles—whether you're dealing with an assertive, detail-oriented boss or a creative, big-picture-oriented colleague—your requests, thoughts, and ideas are more likely to be heard, understood, and acted on.

But the styles conversation isn't just about uncovering other people's styles. There's power in being clear about your own preferences, too, instead of staying silent and wishing people could read your mind. We'll also discuss how to set the tone for how you want others to treat you, how to speak up about your own preferences in a way that's clear and considerate, and what to do when tricky situations come up—because they always do—especially when you're dealing with toxic jerks.

Rather than simply molding yourself to other people's expectations or demanding they adapt to yours, the styles conversation subtly signals your intention to approach others thoughtfully and indicates that you'd appreciate the same in return. The faster you stop taking things personally and find common ground, the sooner you can get on the same wavelength, which means less stress, quicker problem-solving, and fewer headaches.

ID Others' Styles

Studies have found that two primary dimensions shape how people communicate and approach their interactions at work. The first is dominance, which refers to the degree a person attempts to control situations or the thoughts and actions of others, and the second is sociability, which measures how readily someone expresses emotions and prioritizes relationships and emotional connection with others. The intersection of these two dimensions leads to four different styles, which I call the 4Cs. Think of this framework as a shortcut to decoding your boss's behavior without getting swamped by the complexity of human nature.

The Commander

When you work for a Commander, you typically know where you stand and what's expected of you, but Commanders can be so quick to take action that they may steamroll you or others. Because they're low on sociability, these leaders won't be your first pick for a heart-to-heart. They care more about what needs to be done than how everyone feels about it. This doesn't necessarily mean they're uncaring (although they sometimes neglect their team's need for emotional support), but they show their commitment to others by setting clear, ambitious targets rather than through praise or acknowledgment. Expect a brisk work pace with an emphasis on consistent momentum and deadlines.

Don't take it personally if a Commander:

- **Nitpicks your work.** When Commanders challenge your ideas, it's more about stress-testing them to avoid

MOTIVATIONS: results, achieving goals, control, competition, winning
FEARS: wasting time, helplessness, dependence, incompetence, failure
STRENGTHS: confident, direct, decisive, strategic, accountable
WEAKNESSES: impatient, insensitive, overbearing, critical, confrontational

MOTIVATIONS: positivity, popularity, impact, collaboration, experimentation
FEARS: rejection, disapproval, loss of influence, stagnation, negativity
STRENGTHS: open, trusting, optimistic, energetic, visionary
WEAKNESSES: flighty, superficial, overcommitted, difficulty prioritizing, impulsive

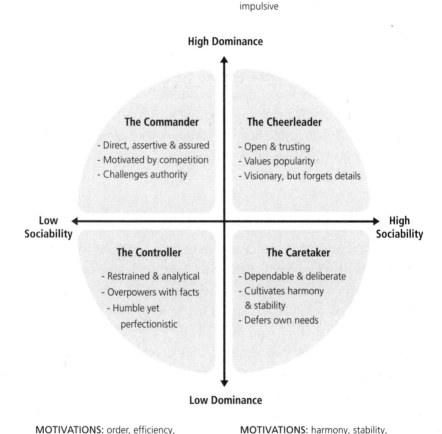

High Dominance

The Commander
- Direct, assertive & assured
- Motivated by competition
- Challenges authority

The Cheerleader
- Open & trusting
- Values popularity
- Visionary, but forgets details

Low Sociability

High Sociability

The Controller
- Restrained & analytical
- Overpowers with facts
- Humble yet perfectionistic

The Caretaker
- Dependable & deliberate
- Cultivates harmony & stability
- Defers own needs

Low Dominance

MOTIVATIONS: order, efficiency, autonomy, accuracy, continuous improvement
FEARS: unpredictability, disarray, spontaneity, vulnerability, mistakes
STRENGTHS: analytical, methodical, disciplined, reserved, determined
WEAKNESSES: rigid, impersonal, demanding, uncreative, uncommunicative

MOTIVATIONS: harmony, stability, connection, giving support, appreciation
FEARS: misunderstandings, overwhelm, change, letting others down, underappreciation
STRENGTHS: calm, empathetic, patient, nurturing, dependable
WEAKNESSES: overprotective, too accommodating, indecisive, conflict-avoidant, risk-averse

mistakes and make them stronger rather than dissatisfaction with you or your performance. Acknowledge their input without getting defensive and refute with solid data: "I see what you mean about the message lacking urgency. We approached it that way because our feedback survey showed . . ." Refer to "What to Do When . . . You Work with a Control Freak" in chapter 1 for more tips on dealing with excess scrutiny.

- **Skips pleasantries and small talk.** Commanders see time as a valuable resource not to be wasted, so respect their desire for efficiency with phrases like "I know you're busy, so let's get right to it" or "I'll dive straight in— here are the key points I'd like to cover." And don't be offended when they send you two-word email replies without asking how your weekend was.

- **Overlooks your opinion.** Commanders often avoid asking for help because they don't want to appear incompetent or needy. But they do appreciate assertiveness, so have a point of view and present it clearly. Start your pitch with something like "I believe . . . ," "My recommendation is . . . ," "From my perspective, it seems that . . . ," "Based on what I've observed, it'd make sense to . . . ," or "Here are my initial thoughts."

- **Selectively delegates.** Driven by their fear of failure and desire for control, Commanders may rely heavily on a few "star players," burdening some and underutilizing others. If you feel sidelined, use the ownership conversation to ask for more responsibilities (chapter 3). If you're overloaded, use the boundaries conversation to push back tactfully (chapter 4).

More tips for managing up to a Commander:

- When writing emails, use direct subject lines (e.g., Project X: Input Required by [date] or Budget Approval for Q3), and keep messages concise. End with a clear call to action: "Please reply yes or no" or "Can you confirm Friday works?"

- Commanders like close oversight, so provide regular, brief project status updates, highlighting progress toward goals or adjustments to stay on track. Avoid too much context. Share your bottom line up front (BLUF), providing your main takeaway or request first.

- Focus your contributions around results, efficiency, and effectiveness. For instance, reframe "I fixed the IT team's workflow problem, and they really appreciated it" to "I got rid of IT's workflow bottleneck, which should increase their task completion rate about 20 percent."

- Be ready to answer questions related to the value and feasibility of your proposals: What's the return on investment? Why should we do this now? What's the competition doing? What's the data to support this? How fast can we get this done?

- Commanders appreciate candor, so bring up conflicts early. "We might be on different pages about [issue] and I think talking about it now will save us trouble down the road" or "I've been thinking about what you said last week, and something isn't sitting quite right. Could we take a few minutes today to revisit that conversation?"

The Cheerleader

A Cheerleader is usually an upbeat people person with a wide range of interests. They're expressive and enjoy sharing stories and feelings, and tend to be energetic, optimistic, and enthusiastic. Like Commanders, Cheerleaders value moving fast and aiming high, but they love building relationships and playing connector, so don't be afraid to ask them to make introductions that expand your own circle. Their focus on team spirit makes for an environment that's positive and fun, but some might find their high-energy, group-oriented style overwhelming. Likewise, the Cheerleader's focus on keeping things hunky-dory and staying "big picture" can lead them to shy away from tough conversations—and you might not always get the nitty-gritty feedback or specific direction you want.

Don't take it personally if a Cheerleader:

- **Cancels meetings at the last minute.** Cheerleader bosses do this because they're juggling too much at once and hate disappointing others they view as influential. Take the lead to reschedule, or you'll be forgotten as they chase the next shiny object. Try this: "I understand your schedule is tight, but we're running out of time to plan for X. So I'll grab twenty minutes on your calendar to connect about that tomorrow unless you let me know otherwise."

- **Changes priorities frequently.** Cheerleaders love to ideate and want to explore every possibility. Their flightiness can be frustrating, but when the Cheerleader thinks of yet another new idea or veers off topic, gently steer them back: "That's fascinating. I'll make a note so we don't lose sight of this and can revisit it at a better time." Be clear about what's achievable, tying it back to team capacity and timelines: "To meet our deadlines and keep the quality of work you're used to, we should stay focused on X."

- **Gives you vague feedback and direction.** Because they thrive on big ideas and broad visions, Cheerleaders prefer to inspire and motivate rather than provide step-by-step instructions. They assume you can fill in the details or worry that being too specific might stifle your creativity. When given vague feedback, drill deeper: "Can you share what success looks like for this project?" Provide options since Cheerleaders sometimes struggle to come up with specifics on their own: "I want to make sure X hits the mark. Here are a few ideas I've come up with. Which one do you feel fits best?"

- **Forgets to follow up or follow through.** Your Cheerleader boss's desire to help may outpace their ability to deliver. To manage this, send polite reminders ("Circling back on the resources for [project]. Any updates?"), ask for timelines ("When can we expect the marketing materials?"), or follow up with summaries ("Here's a recap of our meeting: You agreed to provide X by Wednesday").

More tips for managing up to a Cheerleader:

- Polish your deliverables, particularly anything that will be shared outside your team. Spend more time formatting your reports or practicing your presentations. Your boss will appreciate the effort you put into maintaining their positive image.

- Use words that match their optimistic mindset. For example: "I see an *opportunity* to take [project] to the next level," "There's a lot of *exciting potential* to capitalize on [new trend]," or "I think we *can accomplish even more* if we [idea]—and that we could set a new standard in the company."

- Drive them toward a decision by emphasizing which direction is most popular and who supports it: "The majority of the team prefers Option A because . . ." or "There's consensus from Operations that this is the best way to move forward." Cheerleaders thrive on support and the approval of others.

- Balance professionalism with warmth in meetings. Start with friendly greetings or by sharing a relevant story to break the ice. Incorporate quick polls or roundtable updates to keep energy high. Celebrate your colleagues' contributions and wins, not just your own.

- Bring up a hard conversation they're avoiding by starting and ending on a positive note. This isn't about flattery—it's about making them more receptive to what comes next: "Your ability to motivate the team has been invaluable and I think we can build on that by addressing [challenge] . . . Thanks for chatting about this. I'm excited about the steps we put together."

The Caretaker

Caretakers are patient peacekeepers who listen carefully and make sure everyone feels seen and heard. They pride themselves on being there for others and bringing a calming vibe to everything they do. While they're high on sociability like the Cheerleader, Caretakers are more subdued and nurturing. They want you to feel safe voicing your thoughts and struggles—knowing you're backed by a leader who cares deeply. But at the same time, their indecisiveness can be a drag, particularly in fast-paced or high-stakes environments where quick action and risk-taking are crucial. Plus, if the Caretaker takes a vacation or gets pulled into other projects, the team may completely stall, unsure of how to proceed without constant guidance.

Don't take it personally if a Caretaker:

- **Constantly checks in.** Worried about being underappreciated and not meeting their team's needs, Caretakers sometimes "helicopter" manage or, worse, make you feel like you have to reassure *them* instead of the other way around. Gently make it clear you can handle tasks on your own without them hovering: "I've got this under control, but I'll definitely let you know if I need any help."

- **Hoards work and stretch projects.** Your boss may believe taking on the burden of extra work safeguards you from stress—or they're convinced that they're best suited to handle tasks. To overcome their control issues, propose a gradual transition ("Let's start with me handling part of [project], and we can go from there") or suggest working together initially ("How about we tag-team on [project] at first? That way, you can see my approach and make sure it's on track").

- **Fails to advocate for you.** Caretakers dread confrontation, even if it means not standing up for their team. Help them grow a backbone by providing concrete suggestions along with wording to make speaking up less daunting: "Could you mention [team win] at the next leadership meeting? It'd be great to get more visibility for our work. I drafted a few key points to make it as simple as possible."

- **Drops news on you at the eleventh hour.** In a misdirected effort to keep things calm and stable, your boss may hold back important information, leaving you scrambling. Instead, regularly ask for insight on potential shifts: "Are there any developments we should be aware of? It would help us plan and adjust accordingly" or "Knowing about changes ahead of time helps me prepare, so any heads-up would be helpful."

More tips for managing up to a Caretaker:

- Segue into work topics softly instead of diving straight into business. Start with a personal touch or light conversation: "Hope you had a good weekend! How was the flower show?"

- Don't ask for something without providing the context and your rationale first. The Caretaker wants the full picture before making any decision. Try these approaches: "Before we dive in, let me set the stage for

how we got here . . . ," or "Here are the key factors that
led to X . . . ," or "I'd like to give you an overview of my
thought process . . ."

- Introduce ideas earlier than you might with other types
  of bosses. The Caretaker needs extra time to think it
  over. Make suggestions—not assertions—explicitly
  highlighting how your proposal will affect people's
  feelings. Close with an open-ended question: "The team
  has been stretched and it seems to be impacting
  everyone's mood. Perhaps we could do [idea] to help us
  feel more connected. How would you feel about trying
  this?"

- Nudge them from indecision to action by providing a
  detailed plan. Give them reassurance that you've
  outlined the steps and identified potential risks and
  know how you'll mitigate them: "I understand the value
  of careful consideration and we've done our due
  diligence."

- Emphasize that you see feedback as useful and necessary,
  since the Caretaker will be hesitant to deliver criticism:
  "I feel safe to ask for your honest opinion on my
  performance because I know it comes from a place of
  helping me grow."

The Controller

Controllers excel through their meticulous attention to detail, reli-
ance on data, and a preference for working behind the scenes to
ensure everything runs like clockwork. Facts, stats, and smooth

workflows are their love language. Logical and precise, they want to solve hairy problems with a high degree of accuracy. They tend to be serious and reserved leaders who worry less about social connections and more about optimizing existing standards, rules, and processes. This can be a dream for those who love clear instructions and knowing exactly what to do next. But Controllers can also come off as rigid and restrictive, especially when quick pivots or innovative leaps are needed to stay ahead.

Don't take it personally if a Controller:

- **Rejects your ideas without consideration.** Controllers are wary of new ideas because they see them as risks that could lead to mistakes. So frame ideas as enhancements to existing processes, not as net new changes: "[Idea] builds on our current system . . ." or "We can take what we're already doing and make it even better by . . ."

- **Requires multiple approvals or reviews.** It's not that they don't trust you; rather, they believe that having multiple sets of eyes means standards will be met. Before starting work ask, "What are the key criteria you're looking for in this project? I want to make sure I meet your expectations from the outset." Suggest a quick pre-mortem session to catch any issues early: "Can we check in before I finalize this? I want to address any concerns you might have."

- **Expects you to be an expert in everything.** If your boss overloads you with dense information or complex documentation, turn it back around and ask for guidance on what's most critical: "I appreciate all the details.

What would you say are the key points I should prioritize to make sure we're compliant?"

- **Keeps their distance.** Controllers' tendency to value efficiency over personal connections can be a boon for productivity, but it can also feel cold. Once you accept that your Controller boss may never prioritize team building or magically become the caring mentor who asks about your kids, you free up energy to meet those needs through other connections. Avoid asking personal questions and stick to work-related topics during conversations. They steer clear of discussions about feelings or morale, focusing on tasks and results instead.

More tips for managing up to a Controller:

- Default to a more formal communication style in both written and verbal interactions, respecting their preference for structure and professionalism. Likewise, adhere to the systems and processes your Controller boss has put in place. They value order and predictability, so even if you think another report format might look better, show them you can work within their established frameworks.

- Balance brevity and completeness. Use bullet points or numbered lists in emails to cover the necessities without overwhelming the Controller boss with dense paragraphs (which they may perceive as fluff). Use appendices or attachments, so they have all the details at their fingertips. A line like "For data supporting Option B, see the attached analysis" keeps your messages concise yet comprehensive.

- Controllers respond well to evidence-based discussions, so use data and facts to gain support. Demonstrate your ability to operate independently within the parameters they've set. Before submitting a deliverable to a client, for instance, run through the quality check provided by your boss.

- Schedule meetings to give feedback—no drop-ins or drive-bys. Focus on concrete, observable examples versus your subjective opinion. Propose changes that can be integrated into new or existing systems or processes: "With the volume of emails we get, I'd suggest we set up an internal categorization to label messages by project and urgency."

- When the Controller gets mired in detail, share specific examples or scenarios to illustrate the tangible consequences of not making timely decisions. Get them to comprehend the human impact they may neglect or overlook with stats or findings that underscore how certain decisions could affect (or have affected) morale, turnover rates, or engagement: "Our survey showed a 30 percent increase in team satisfaction when we did X."

While the 4Cs can be an incredibly helpful guide to decoding your boss's style, it's not unusual for someone to embody traits of two adjacent styles, like a Caretaker boss who is obsessed with structure and spreadsheets (Controller tendencies). And though it's less common, it's not impossible for someone to share traits across diagonally opposite styles—like a Controller having moments of being a Cheerleader. You might not always like or agree with your boss's approach—that's normal—but if there comes a point where their actions become disruptive to you or others, it's not enough to say, "Oh, that's just how they are!" Ultimately, personal style doesn't give anyone a pass to be a jerk, so we'll cover how to decide to speak up about harmful behaviors later in the chapter.

The key is to stay flexible and observant, adjusting your strategies as you learn more about your boss's preferences and behaviors. Because even if your relationships are strong, they can always be *better*. This goes for your co-workers, too. For instance, Elise, a program manager at a nonprofit, recognized that Prashant, her counterpart on the fundraising team, was a classic Caretaker who preferred focusing on proven campaigns rather than testing new approaches. So when Elise wanted to persuade Prashant to generate funding for a new, more experimental initiative, she focused on how it would minimize risk, maximize predictability, and maintain relationships with their donors. By tailoring her approach, Elise didn't just coexist with or passively tolerate Prashant, she made him feel deeply understood.

Create Your Me Manual

Now that you've identified your manager's communication style, let's do a deep dive on your own and create what I call a "Me Manual." This exercise brings a game-changing level of internal clarity, even if you never explicitly share your preferences with anyone else. For example, do you process information better through visuals, emails, or verbal explanations? When making decisions, do you rely more on data and analysis or intuition and experience? Do you feel more energized after group brainstorming sessions or solo deep-work sprints? Your answers to these questions will give you a clear understanding of what you need to perform at your best so you can subtly steer your relationships in that direction.

Understanding your own style also helps you pinpoint what bothers you at work and find solutions. For instance, if you thrive on bouncing ideas off others and your workplace relies on siloed, email-based communication, you might feel stifled and disconnected. Recognizing this lets you address the issue and find workarounds, like setting up virtual coffee chats to satisfy your need for spontaneous, creative discussions. Or maybe you do best with direct, no-nonsense communication. By letting a Caretaker boss know up front that you prefer receiving feedback in writing with specific examples, you can avoid the frustration of vague, sugarcoated critiques that leave you unsure of what you can do to improve.

But it's not just about you. When your manager understands your preferred ways of communicating, they can get the best out of you. They're not left guessing how to assign tasks that play to your strengths or bring up disagreements. It's a win-win: You get the support you need and they see better results from you, which makes them look good. The human brain is designed to conserve energy and effort, which is why many leaders tell me it's a relief when their employees are up-front about how to manage them. One engineering manager told me, "I love it when my team is forthcoming about how they work best. I need them to tell me how I can put them in a position for success."

So grab a journal and a pen or open a digital doc and reflect on the following questions. For now, your responses are for your eyes only. You can find a fillable Me Manual template on my website at managingup.com/bonuses.

Information processing

- Do I understand and remember concepts better through visuals, the written word, or verbal explanations?

- When making decisions, do I rely more on data and analysis or intuition and experience?

- Am I more comfortable sharing my thoughts in a meeting, through an email, or in a one-on-one conversation?

- When learning something new, do I benefit more from group discussions where different perspectives are shared, or do I prefer to digest the information on my own first?

- How often do I like to get updates or check-ins on projects? In what format and via what channels?

- Do I prefer to receive information in concise summaries to get the gist, or do I like in-depth explanations that allow me to grasp nuance?

Task management

- Am I drawn to long-term, detailed projects, or do I enjoy quick sprints?

- Do I prefer projects that center on a single topic or those that allow me to explore a broad range of subjects?

- Do I like to tackle tasks in sequential order, or do I prefer jumping around?

- Which organizational tools or systems have I found most effective, and why do they work for me?

- What motivates me to start a new task—external deadlines, personal interest, or something else?

- Do I prefer having all information before making decisions, or am I comfortable with some ambiguity?

Work environment and schedule

- What time do I usually start and end work?

- How much daily interaction with colleagues do I need to feel engaged and motivated?

- To what extent do I need quiet or dedicated "deep work" blocks to concentrate?

- How does working from home or remotely affect my productivity and satisfaction compared to being in the office?

- Beyond just morning or evening, what specific times of day do I notice peaks and troughs in my energy and focus levels?

- What times of day or the week work best for certain types of meetings—brainstorming, status updates, one-on-ones, etc.?

- What are my boundaries regarding work communication and tasks outside of standard working hours?

Feedback and conflict

- How do I like to receive feedback? Written, verbally, in private? How important are specific examples and actionable advice?

- Do I respond better to feedback presented in a straightforward manner, or do I prefer a more empathetic tone?

- Would I grow more from regular, periodic feedback, or am I fine receiving input on an as-needed basis?

- Do I tend to address conflict head-on as soon as it arises, or do I prefer to take time to reflect and prepare before tackling the issue?

- In a team disagreement, do I find myself more focused on the content of the conflict or the emotions and relationships involved?

- How do I see my role in team dynamics? Do I see myself as a mediator, an advocate, or perhaps as a neutral party trying to maintain balance?

Star or highlight responses that are a "must-have" versus a preference. For example, you may *prefer* to get questions in advance of meetings, but it may not be a deal-breaker. On the other hand, going into the office at least a few days a week for real-time collaboration may be a nonnegotiable you need to feel fulfilled. This can help you prioritize what you share and when, which we'll tackle next, as well as how committed you should be about getting a particular need met. I suggest revisiting your Me Manual once a year to keep it fresh as you, your role, and your organization evolve.

Selectively—and Strategically—Share

If you're lucky, you might work for a boss or an organization that welcomes explicit conversations about *how* people work together. One of my clients works at a Big Three management consultancy, and when she's assigned to a new project (and new manager) every six to eight weeks, she speeds up her onboarding and trust building exponentially by walking her leader through her Me Manual so they know how to get the best performance out of her. My client can be that bold because the styles conversation is baked into the company's culture.

But in most cases, you'll have to be more selective and strategic about how, when, and where you choose to disclose and assert your needs, since being so open about them isn't the norm. Plopping a list of demands down on your boss's desk is a surefire way to be written off as self-involved, so go slow and feel the situation out. Share one or two key insights from your Me Manual as a litmus test. Pick preferences that are relatively low stakes, meaning they're not likely to cause disruptions or require significant changes from your boss or anyone else. For example, your manager may have no problem with you working all day with headphones on, but asking the entire team to switch to a new collaboration platform just because you like it isn't going to fly.

If your boss has been open about their own work preferences, it might feel more natural to share your own: "You've mentioned the importance of work-life balance in our team meetings. I've found that having the flexibility to start my day earlier helps me focus. It also means I can be done in time to pick up my kids. Could we see about adjusting my schedule to accommodate this?" You can also seamlessly float your request by:

- **Relating it to a recent success.** "We brought the last deliverable in under budget, and I realized that was possible because of the written briefs you provided and regular touch-bases we had. That kind of structured communication works wonders for me. What do you think about using that same approach for our next project?"

- **Anticipating a change or development.** "Since our deliverables will be picking up next quarter, I'm planning to set aside at least one hour a day for heads-down work to make sure I stay on top of everything. I'll block off that time starting Monday, unless I hear otherwise."

- **Proposing your preference as a solution to a problem.** "I've noticed our one-on-ones usually run over, which means we're both late for our next meetings. Having a clear agenda could make a huge difference. Mind if we try that? I'll be in charge of putting it together."

Though it may feel nerve-racking to express your needs so directly, clarity—especially when it's done in service of your boss's and the team's goals—can lead people to trust and like you more because it eases their workload and stress.

Optimize Your Interactions

Sharing your work and communication preferences is more than just an act of courage—it's a psychological transaction. According to social exchange theory, people try to maximize the rewards they get from a relationship and minimize the costs, something called the minimax principle. That means every time your boss says yes to a small change and sees a positive outcome from accommodating you, you'll set the stage for a bigger, broader version of the styles conversation during which they're more likely to be amenable to future requests. Frame this discussion as an opportunity to build on the positive developments and value that have come before: "We've seen great changes from some of the adjustments we've made so far, so I'm hoping we could have a deeper conversation about how we can continue to optimize how we work with each other."

You might also look for a natural transition point to justify broaching the topic, like the beginning of a new year or quarter: "December is here, and I'm thinking about how to set myself and the team up for success next year. I'd be able to deliver at a higher level if I had more insight into how you work. Could we reserve some time to discuss?" Or perhaps you introduce the topic at the start of a new project: "We haven't discussed in-depth how we prefer to communicate yet. Knowing things like how and when you want to receive updates or how you like to receive feedback would be helpful. Would you be open to chatting about this?"

When the time comes, kick off the discussion with something like this: "Some of the changes we've implemented recently, like [specific preference], have really paid off. I've noticed [positive outcome], which I think has made a big difference. It's been great seeing how small adjustments can have such a big impact for both of us. This got me thinking about how we could take things a step further and really dial in to how we work together. I've got some ideas around this and would love to get your input as well. How does that sound?"

You might offer to walk your boss through a certain category within your Me Manual (e.g., "I'd really like to get on the same page about how we share information with each other") or focus on a cross section of different categories in the context of a certain project, client, or initiative (e.g., "Let's talk through the Acme project—not just how we share updates, but also outlining my work schedule over the next three months"). Hear your boss out and work through how you can mesh your preferences with their goals, desires, and constraints. For example, try asking one or more of the following questions:

- What are your thoughts on what I've shared? Do you see any immediate concerns or benefits from your side?

- How do you think we can integrate these ideas without disrupting our current workflow too much?

- Which of these changes do you think we should tackle first? Are there any you believe would have the most impact?

- Are there any work or communication adjustments that you think would help us work better together?

While we hope for the best, not every boss will take these conversations well. If you get a less than helpful response, here's how to handle the most typical reactions:

- **Your manager seems offended.** "My request wasn't meant to be a criticism about how we do things. But I've noticed I bring better ideas to the table when I have time to prepare. I see the value of impromptu meetings under certain circumstances, but I'm hoping we can find a middle ground so I can contribute more."

- **Your manager is hesitant.** "I definitely get your concern about fairness. Maybe we could set up very clear guidelines for remote work eligibility that are tied to specific projects or tasks. That way, it's less likely to be perceived as special treatment."

- **Your manager outright says no.** "Understood, we need to keep things moving quickly and on-the-go feedback is the standard. It's just that details often get lost in the rush for me. If speaking privately isn't an option, could we set aside a few minutes for a quick recap at the end of the day or week? That would give me a chance to clarify what you want me to change."

Flex, Don't Fawn

Ultimately, the styles conversation with your boss—or anyone else with power for that matter—is about being clear and assertive regarding what you need to thrive, while also recognizing they hold the reins in many ways. Matching your boss's style will create rapport and connection, but the idea is to flex, not fawn, making small concessions to your own style in order to get better results without abandoning yourself or ignoring who you are at your core.

In chapter 1, we talked about mirroring or repeating the last few words someone else says in order to dig deeper, affirm their thoughts and opinions, and confirm you're listening. You can take this a step further into the physical realm by using similar manner-isms, pacing, or language during conversation, which serves as a social glue, activating the rewards area of that person's brain. This doesn't mean mimicking people's behavior like a puppet, which they would likely perceive as creepy or as mockery. Instead, it's about observing someone's communication style and thoughtfully adjusting the way you show up by amplifying certain aspects of your personality.

Flexing, when done right, supercharges your communication and makes others feel understood. For instance, let's say you're an excitable "let's do all the things!" Cheerleader type working under a Caretaker. In trying to convince them to take a course of action, you stay true to yourself by emphasizing the positive im-pact of your ideas and adopting a motivating tone, but you can also accommodate your Caretaker boss by slowing down, allow-ing them to process, and making space for their questions (e.g., "Before I give you more details, let's pause. What concerns do you have?").

Flexing also means filling in your own strengths where others have gaps. When Alex, a sales director and Commander, was tasked with collaborating with a cross-functional team of mostly Control-lers, he quickly realized the group's penchant for precision was compromising their ability to meet deadlines. When the team en-countered critical choices, Alex stepped up and offered straight-forward recommendations, which short-circuited analysis paralysis and ensured projects stayed on track. And when unforeseen chal-lenges arose and the Controllers were inclined to stick to pre-defined processes, Alex was open to alternative solutions. This flexibility often meant saved time and resources.

Beyond the Conversation

Keep Your Eyes Open

No styles conversation can touch every detail of how people work. Observe how your boss and colleagues in leadership positions interact with team members as well. In particular, look for clues among the actions of your team's highest performers and replicate them for yourself. For example, do they drop by your manager's office versus delivering news via email? Are there specific phrases or language they use consistently that resonates well with others?

Likewise, don't be afraid to ask your colleagues to share examples of things they've done to successfully meet your boss's needs in the past. You'll quickly see there are many common denominators, and these practices are the ones you'll want to consistently adopt. Here are a few sample questions:

- When it comes to decision-making, have you noticed any patterns in how our boss prefers to be involved or informed?

- What has been successful in terms of providing input to our boss and how have you ensured it's well received?

- Are there any unwritten rules or cultural nuances that are particularly important to our manager?

- In discussions or meetings where our boss is present, what nonverbal cues or body language have you noticed that show their level of interest or approval?

- How do you seek clarification from our boss without appearing indecisive or lacking confidence? What techniques work for getting the guidance you need?

Finally, consider your most successful interactions with your manager. What do you think made those interactions beneficial? Consider the level of formality, clarity of messaging, and the balance between providing information and seeking input.

Discern Digital Body Language

Today when roughly half of the workweek is spent communicating digitally, it's important to pay attention to the subtle cues that make up "digital body language," as author Erica Dhawan calls it. This includes adjusting to preferences around:

- the use of emojis or punctuation such as exclamation points, periods, ellipses, and ALL CAPS;

- response time and how that relates to levels of urgency or respect (e.g., Are delayed responses equivalent to ignoring someone?);

- the choice of medium—phone call, meeting, text message, etc.;

- whether they use formal openings and closings to messages as well as Reply All and cc tendencies.

When Emanuel, a research assistant, noticed that his boss often wrote emails in bullet points, he began writing in bullet points, too. After a while, Emanuel asked his manager, "It seems you prefer when I list out items in an email. Am I on track? Is that something you'd like me to continue doing?" To which his manager responded, "Yes, the numbering and bullets make it so much easier for me to scan." Geraldine, a graphic designer who adored structure, had an account executive who was more of a free spirit. When Geraldine left more room for discussion during their meetings, their relationship blossomed.

What to Do When . . .

You're Unsure If Your Manager's Behavior Is a Quirk— or a Red Flag

Maybe your boss often shoots down ideas or seems chronically indecisive. Perhaps they rarely, if ever, tell you you're doing a good job. If you're questioning whether your boss's actions are simply an annoying idiosyncrasy or a red flag, don't worry just yet. In a moment, I'll give you tactics for dealing with toxic jerks, and in chapter 5, you'll discover how to diplomatically give feedback that actually gets acted upon.

- **Label problematic behaviors, not people.** While it's tempting to throw up your hands and say, "My boss sucks!" or "My leaders have no idea how to explain things clearly!," don't immediately cast judgment. Instead, get curious and assume positive intent. If you can uncover the prior history, circumstances, needs, wants, or stressors lurking behind certain behaviors, you can be more objective.

- **Try making small adjustments.** If your boss gets irritated when you give a lot of backstory, try leading with your main point first. Cutting to the chase can prevent your boss from losing patience, making conversations less stressful for both of you. But sometimes all the tweaks in the world don't help—and you need to take further action.

- **Keep tabs on the negative impact.** Let's say your manager gets excited about new projects. One week they're pushing for innovation and the next for cutting costs. Their enthusiasm, while commendable, leaves you scrambling, unable to complete anything thoroughly or meet shifting expectations, which can hurt you—and them—in the long run.

- **Note whether the annoyance expands beyond you.** If so, it's escalated from a style difference to a disruptive pattern worth addressing. One of my clients was getting really frustrated because her boss refused to update an obsolete procedure. She knew she needed to say something when other teams started complaining about how her boss's rigidity was messing up their workflows, too.

- **Weigh what's at stake if you let things slide.** If the behavior continues as is for another three months, six months, or a year, how does it affect your future? Maybe you realize that working for someone who withholds praise won't be good for your mental health in the long term. Or perhaps you see that your boss's indecisiveness is stopping you from meeting deadlines, which could harm your reputation and career prospects.

You're Actually Dealing with a Toxic Jerk

There's a difference between a *challenging* boss and an abusive one who constantly undermines your dignity (personal insults,

public humiliation, threats about job security, withholding information, credit hoarding, scapegoating, favoritism, etc.). I once
worked for the CEO of a small tech startup who was quick to
anger, deflected blame, and shouted in meetings when he didn't
like something. Hopefully you'll never work for (or with) someone like this, but if you do, here's how I dealt with it in the short
term while I devised my escape plan, which we'll talk more about
in chapter 10:

- **Prioritize self-preservation.** Lessen the duration and
  frequency of your one-on-ones, or better yet, switch to
  email updates (where possible) so you don't have to
  meet in person and you can create a paper trail. Avoid
  hallway conversations, lunches, or events with them you
  aren't required to attend. I began working from home
  and taking more onsite customer meetings, which
  allowed me to get away from the office and the CEO's
  wrath.

- **Identify safe spots.** Look for situations in which a difficult
  boss or colleague wouldn't want to show their true
  colors. If you need to discuss a sensitive topic with your
  boss, try to do it in a meeting where others are present,
  or even in a semipublic place like the office coffee area.
  Their desire to maintain a certain image with people
  might keep their bad behavior in check.

- **Gray-rock it.** Toxic people, especially the narcissistic kind,
  love to say and do things to get a rise out of you.
  Counter this by being a gray rock, which is a strategy
  that refers to being bland, boring, and nonreactive. I
  began keeping my conversations with my CEO short

and sweet (not giving away any personal information), keeping my face neutral when he made snide remarks, and avoiding eye contact during meetings. While it felt rude and unnatural, he eventually lost interest in targeting me with his tirades.

- **Find humor, or pity, when they act out.** Although it may not feel like it in the moment, 99 percent of the time a person's reaction is about their emotional immaturity, not necessarily something you said or did. Some of my clients find it helpful to picture their terrible boss as a scared child. Others imagine their manager's mean comments in a silly voice, which helps diffuse their power.

- **Protect your energy.** To disconnect at the end of the day, try an exercise I call "the backpack." In your mind's eye, put stressful situations from your day into an imaginary backpack that you shrug off and leave in the corner of your office overnight. Make this exercise concrete by drawing a square on paper and scribbling down your concerns. Tear up the paper and throw it away, symbolically letting go of the situation as you do.

While you might assume it'd be easier to have bosses and colleagues who share your communication preferences, diverse teams are actually more innovative and get better results than homogeneous ones. Knowing how to mesh well with a mix of personalities won't just make your work life smoother, it will also give you a competitive edge. Hopefully you've started on your Me Manual—maybe you've even begun sharing your preferences with your boss or others! If not, start by simply observing your own patterns as well as the idiosyncrasies of those above and across from you. By mastering interpersonal nuances you've discovered in this chapter, you reduce friction and misunderstandings, which means less time fixing mix-ups and more time getting meaningful work done.

CHAPTER THREE

The Ownership Conversation

Seize opportunities without stepping on toes

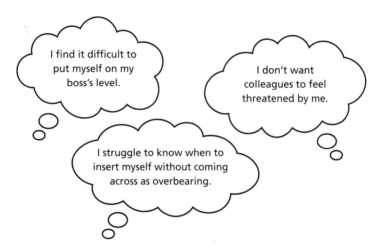

The hospital where Seiko worked had been under siege from Covid-19 for more than two years. Everyone—from physicians to nurses to allied health professionals like Seiko—was stretched thin. As a certified prosthetist orthotist, Seiko spent long days fitting people with braces, splints, and prosthetic devices, but she and her colleagues were still working overtime to serve a backlog of patients whose appointments and procedures had been delayed by the pandemic.

One day Seiko came to our coaching session frustrated by a bottleneck that caused patients to suffer with pain for far longer than necessary. Because her clinic didn't have its own mailing address, incoming shipments of orthotic and prosthetic devices were often delivered to the wrong department and went missing for days. For someone with a broken limb, arthritic back, or difficulty walking, a delay could be excruciating.

"All of my colleagues complain about mailing issues, but no one wants to step up and do something. They think that dealing with the mail is grunt work."

"What about you? What if you turned this annoyance into an opportunity?" I asked, which got Seiko thinking about how she could tackle the challenge.

The department was so overwhelmed that Seiko realized she had to start small. She recognized that her boss, the head of the clinic, might not be aware of the postal problem. She prepared a three-question survey for clinic employees, asking if they had experienced a delay in patient care; if so, for how long; and if they had a story to share. More than 80 percent had had a mail room issue, and after two weeks, Seiko had nine stories of the ways in which it had negatively impacted the clinic.

Seiko's boss was shocked, but also so busy that he was happy to let her take the lead. Unfortunately, during the first few months, Seiko met resistance from the hospital's leadership. The fallout from the pandemic had been so severe that a new mailing address seemed insignificant, but Seiko secured an invite to the next monthly interdepartmental meeting to present the data she'd gathered along with the research she'd done on how to establish a separate address. After that meeting, the administrators finally agreed that Seiko should move ahead.

Though the approval process took more than a year of navigating bureaucratic red tape, the clinic eventually received its own address. Within weeks, an influx of positive online reviews arrived and generated both referrals from doctors' offices and greater revenue. The boost in patient satisfaction was possible because Seiko had identified a worthwhile problem, built buy-in, and acted like an owner. As hospital operations began returning to normal, the head of the clinic started bringing Seiko in on more strategic conversations, since he saw firsthand her ability to get complex things done.

Seiko discovered that if you wait around for others to grant you greater influence or opportunities—or for things to magically change at work—you might be waiting a long time. *The ownership conversation* changes that, allowing you to solve problems that make your own job difficult or frustrating. It's your chance to spot and seize challenges, propose solutions, and execute on your ideas so you can do better work with greater autonomy. For example, consider a graphic designer who's constantly frustrated by last-minute requests from the sales team. These rush jobs not only force her to deliver subpar work but also throw off her carefully planned schedule week after week. Instead of silently seething or complaining to colleagues, she could talk with the sales manager to understand the root cause of the last-minute tasks. Together, they might put in place a new planning process for requests that creates more reasonable deadlines. Or imagine a data analyst who spends hours each week manually updating dashboards because the current system is clunky and outdated. Rather than accepting this inefficiency as "just the way things are," they research automated solutions and pitch it to their manager. By taking ownership of the problem and presenting a compelling case for change, they free up significant time and mental energy.

Of course, not every problem can be solved overnight, and some issues may be beyond your direct control. Plus, every boss might not respond as positively as Seiko's. That's why in this chapter, you'll learn to solve the *right* problems, get your manager and others on board, and take thoughtful action in a way that minimizes resistance.

If you've been told to "stay in your lane" and follow orders at work, then it may come as a surprise to know that ownership skills rank among the top ten most important attributes employers want, according to the World Economic Forum's *Future of Jobs Report*. But ownership isn't just beneficial for organizations. When you operate in this type of "mastery climate"—one characterized by learning and genuine enjoyment of the work—you're more likely to feel fulfilled and satisfied. The ownership conversation, then, is one of the best ways to take charge of your circumstances. Instead of feeling defeated, angry, or simply reacting to whatever comes your way, you're essentially saying, "I'm not going to be at the mercy of this situation; I'm going to be the solution."

Identify a Worthwhile Issue

There's no shortage of problems to solve at work, whether you want to streamline a convoluted workflow, pitch new product concepts, introduce training to fill a team-wide skills gap, take the lead in addressing a cross-functional conflict that's holding up approvals, solve a safety hazard, initiate knowledge sharing across departments—the list goes on and on. But all challenges are not created equal. So before you act, survey the landscape. The best issues to address are ones that simultaneously lower your own work stress *and* that of your manager or other influential colleagues. After all, if you can solve people's pain points, you'll position yourself as a strategic contributor and garner the attention of important decision-makers.

Let's look at five types of problems that are worth actively ad-dressing, starting with the tactical and moving to the more future-looking. See if any of the persistent issues in your workplace fall into one of these categories.

Worthwhile Problems	What to Ask Yourself	Common Situations	Ownership in Action
1. Bothersome Bottlenecks	What issues or inefficiencies are causing headaches and slowing down progress and productivity?	• Approval, hiring, or resource delays • Technical issues and missing or broken equipment • Manual processes and lack of access to data	New hires are taking too long to get up to speed. You take it upon yourself to create an onboarding manual to streamline knowledge transfer.
2. Neglected Needs	What unmet needs, projects, or priorities are currently overlooked and under-addressed?	• Team training gaps • Customer experience upgrades • Satisfying new regulations	When your company acquires another firm, you see a hole to be filled in reconciling lingering due-diligence matters.

Worthwhile Problems	What to Ask Yourself	Common Situations	Ownership in Action
3. Feedback Patterns	What are our team members, customers, clients, or constituents saying they'd like more or less of?	• Too many meetings • Product improvements • Knowledge-sharing barriers	You design and circulate a spreadsheet tracker after several of your teammates complain about difficulties managing bugs in your company's software.
4. Upcoming Projects	What's in the pipeline and how can I be a step ahead?	• Creating new systems or documentation • Forecasting, planning, and needs assessments • Stakeholder outreach	Your team is launching a new website next month. You prep several weeks' worth of blog articles ahead of time.
5. Innovation Opportunities	How can we reimagine, add to, or evolve our work to improve results?	• Strategic partnerships • Expanding into different markets • Creating new services	Observing the need for specialized skills in your organization, you propose setting up an internship program with a local university.

Though it may feel as if bothersome bottlenecks and neglected needs are easy to tackle regardless of positional power, as in Seiko's case, these kinds of persistent issues often linger because they're less glamorous than introducing a new idea or innovation. On the other hand, feedback patterns, upcoming projects, and innovation opportunities tend to require a careful approach because of their external-facing nature and their potential impact on other teams and departments.

Build Buy-In

No matter the worthwhile issue you choose, taking ownership requires having enough grit to navigate office politics, competing agendas, and organizational inertia (e.g., "Well, that's how we've always done it"). The surest way to ruffle feathers and be labeled disruptive is to come out of nowhere and demand or implement a sweeping change. At the same time, you'll never make any headway or show your boss what you're capable of if you stop and ask permission every time you want to go beyond your job description and responsibilities. The counterintuitive truth of the ownership conversation is this: Having a good idea is just the starting point. You need to get everyone on board and overcome resistance to make real progress.

Pre-suade to Set the Stage

How you approach the critical moments or days *before* you take action will have a dramatic effect on how quickly your boss warms up to a concept or whether you face knee-jerk resistance. Pre-suasion, a term coined by Dr. Robert Cialdini, the godfather of modern influence, involves leveraging the psychological concept of priming to subtly influence the perceptions and attitudes in your audience (your boss, other superiors, and colleagues) so that when you do take initiative, it's received in the best possible light. Pre-suading lays the groundwork for your ask, making initial changes and subsequent steps feel like a sensible progression rather than a jarring leap.

Here's what pre-suading looks like in action:

- **Seek feedback.** Before suggesting a new communication tool, ask colleagues for feedback on current ones, which can make your proposal to your boss seem like a natural evolution of an ongoing conversation. If you're pitching a work-from-home policy, send out a poll or survey with questions about current frustrations or aspirations around flexibility to prime your superiors and your colleagues for change.

- **Trigger FOMO.** Show how competitors have seen significant growth with similar approaches: "I noticed Company Y recently revamped their process in this area. It got me thinking about our system." Or introduce an idea as something exclusive or time-sensitive to pique interest and urgency: "I've come across an opportunity that might not be around for long . . ."

- **Tease your thoughts.** Hint that you've been researching solutions, encouraging your manager to consider the issue more seriously: "I recently spoke with marketing and learned how they tackled X, and I think we can learn from their approach." Or "I've stumbled upon some interesting solutions to our challenge of Y. Can't wait to share and get your thoughts!"

- **Highlight past successes.** Tie new ideas to past successful projects or familiar strategies to reduce uncertainty. That can sound like "Remember how well it worked to automate our data entry last year? I think we could follow the same approach for our reporting system." Or "Reflecting back on our success with the launch event last year, I'm inspired to get a jump start on our upcoming annual meeting. I have some ideas to infuse the same energy into that event."

- **Pull pain and pleasure levers.** Frame your idea in terms of how it might alleviate interruptions, stress, or confusion (pain) or increase productivity, clarity, or satisfaction (pleasure). For instance, when proposing a new project management tool, explain how it can save hours of tedious work each week, reducing stress (pain) and allowing more time for creative, high-impact tasks (pleasure).

- **Incorporate shared values.** Discuss the company's or team's core vision or mission statement. Once those are fresh in someone's mind, introduce your initiative as an embodiment of those values: "Our customers are top priority. A few of them have been nudging us about our response times. I've sketched out a game plan to tackle that head-on."

- **Engage the senses.** Pitching a wellness initiative? Instead of the usual conference room, use a comfortable lounge.

Soft furnishings, ambient music, and dimmed lighting can evoke a sense of calm and a willingness to be receptive to new ideas. During a presentation on performance milestones, use images of individuals scaling summits or crossing finish lines to symbolize achievement.

Offer a Path Forward

To help you and your idea stand out even more—and increase the chance of it actually being executed—present it with a potential solution. Even if you're venturing into unfamiliar territory, a sound, well-thought-out plan signals competence. It proves you can dissect complex situations and clarifies your intentions, which will set your manager at ease.

Start small, leveraging the foot-in-the-door technique. Proposing an overhaul of your company's entire inventory process, for example, could raise people's hackles. Instead, introduce manageable changes that are easier for people to embrace, like phasing in a few new features to start. You could also suggest a trial period, for example, after which everyone reassesses whether to proceed or go back to business as usual.

Try the SCQA format to help structure your ideas in a way that makes it easier for your boss or anyone else to say yes. This framework allows you to provide context (*situation*), introduce challenges or obstacles (*complication*), pose your hypothesis or questions you considered (*question*), and offer a clear and concise answer or solution (*answer*).

- *Situation*. Revenue has been dipping for two years. Marketing thinks sales isn't pushing products enough.

Sales thinks marketing is out of touch. Tensions are
high, and our numbers are suffering.

- *Complication.* Communication between the departments
  is nonexistent. The sales team is creating their own
  promotional materials. Meanwhile, marketing feels their
  efforts are going to waste. This rift is affecting morale,
  productivity, and most important, the bottom line.

- *Question.* I've been thinking, "How do we get sales and
  marketing on the same page again? And, oh yeah, fix our
  declining numbers?"

- *Answer.* I suggest we arrange a workshop with
  representatives from both teams. This is about
  understanding, not finger-pointing. I'm happy to
  facilitate and lead everyone through some role-reversal
  exercises and scenario planning.

Though it may take practice to implement this framework, it will
soon become second nature as you train yourself to see problems—
and their solutions—through a more logical, action-oriented lens.

STEAL THESE SCRIPTS

Use the following scripts, ranked in order from least assertive to
most assertive, to introduce your ideas, get buy-in from others,
and inform them of your intentions.

- I've noticed an opportunity to make our [process/project] better.
  Would you be open to hearing my thoughts?

- On a scale from 1 to 10, how open would you be to considering a new approach to [task/project]?

- What are your thoughts on trying [new idea]? I believe it'd offer [benefits], and I would love to address your reservations up front.

- I want to ensure I'm not stepping on any toes. Are there any concerns if I pursue [idea]?

- I'm thinking of making a change to [process/project]. Any advice or insights I should consider?

- This approach worked well in [previous scenario]. Think it might apply here, too?

- I've weighed the potential risks and believe we can manage them by [strategy]. Does that sound reasonable?

- Would you object to me moving ahead with [new idea]?

- I've spotted an opportunity in [area/process]. I'm planning to take the lead on it.

- While I'm taking the lead on [task], I'm always open to insights.

- For clarity, I intend to drive [project]. It'd be great to have your support as I move forward.

- I've got a solid handle on [issue/task] and will be taking the reins on it.

- Just so everyone's in the loop, I'm taking ownership of [area/task].

- I believe I can make a difference with [task], so I'm stepping in.

- Given my experience with [area], I'll take the lead on [task].

- To get ahead of [issue], I'll be the one pushing this forward.

- I'll be heading up [project] to ensure we don't duplicate efforts.

Bring Others Along

Taking action is just the starting point. The real work—and reward—comes from the ongoing process of engaging others and keeping them in the loop. Enter the concept of operational transparency. Open loops make the brain work overtime and trigger a stress response, which can cause anxiety and defensiveness. But when you let your manager and others into your process and consistently update them on your progress, it satisfies an innate human need for control and closure. Plus, when people are able to provide feedback or simply observe what's happening, they feel like critical participants rather than just bystanders, making them more trusting, motivated, and satisfied.

Beware of overwhelming people, and experiment with the level of detail depending on your audience. This might include:

- sharing a comparison chart that specifies why one option was chosen over the others based on factors like features, cost, and usability;

- creating a real-time dashboard where anyone can pop in to see key metrics;

- putting up a physical progress bar that acts as a visual reminder and conversation starter about the gains you and your team have made;

- sending out an email at the end of each week to share updates on what you've achieved, the challenges you've faced, and your plans for the upcoming week;

- including an appendix or margin notes that explain your thought processes, your decisions, or the alternative methods you consider whenever you submit a document or report;

- running workshops that simulate parts of your work process to give others hands-on insight into the complexities and intricacies of your tasks.

While your focus is to reveal the "how" and "why" behind your actions, operational transparency sets the stage for greater visibility through openly discussing your accomplishments (which we'll cover in depth in chapter 7). But remember to give others credit where it's due. Perhaps you create a shout-outs slide that highlights key contributors and their roles, or you use footnotes or sidenotes in your reports to attribute specific findings, ideas, or solutions to specific team members. Another option might be to color-code dashboards to visually represent who did what.

Beyond the Conversation

Play to Your Strengths

When Citicorp and Travelers merged in the late 1990s, they approached Paula Scher and her agency Pentagram to design a logo for the new entity and its consumer arm, Citibank. As the banking executives described the goals and challenges of the merger, Paula doodled, and after five minutes, she passed the napkin across the table. "This is your logo." The confidence, expertise, and talent Paula demonstrated in that moment was thanks to twenty years of focused branding and creative practice.

The things that come easily to you are your strengths, so don't discount them because they feel innate. This is called unconscious competence, or when you can perform a skill to such a high degree of mastery that it feels second nature. A study by Gallup found that people who use their strengths every day are three times more likely to report having an excellent quality of life, six times more likely to be engaged at work, and almost 10 percent more productive. Consider what tasks or decisions come effortlessly to you. Creating compelling copy? Negotiating community partnerships? Identifying emerging trends? Jot these down and find opportunities to exercise them alongside taking ownership. Likewise, look for others with complementary strengths and collaborate. For example, you might be a skilled listener who expertly draws insights from client conversations. You can partner with a colleague who is a magnetic presenter and craft your findings into a compelling narrative.

Communicate Like a Pro

When the average attention span is less than ninety seconds, it's critical to get to the point fast. If you present a long, rambling proposal, your boss, other upper management, or even your colleagues may assume you're disorganized and have no idea what you're doing. On the other hand, if you share your ideas succinctly, you demonstrate mastery and confidence and are more likely to be taken seriously.

Here are some of my favorite tips for concise communication—written or spoken:

- Reduce the risk of getting sidetracked by drafting three to five points you want to make.

- Add an executive summary to your written reports to make the information scannable and reinforce key highlights.

- Use bullets and numbering to break down complex concepts into digestible pieces.

- Organize and present your ideas as pillars, steps, or keys so they're easy for your audience (and you) to remember.

- Leverage the center-stage effect, positioning your proposed solution as the middle of three options.

- Swap weak verbs (give, make, do, get, go) for power verbs (analyze, examine, devise, craft, achieve, accelerate).

When choosing a medium, ask yourself: *Is this topic sensitive or controversial? Will it take more than five sentences to explain in writing and require a lot of back-and-forth?* If the answer to either of these questions is yes, then find a way to have a call or meet in person. This ensures confidentiality (to a certain extent) and allows you to take nonverbal cues into account. Ditto for when a matter requires immediate attention. You want a real-time exchange, quick decisions, and an empathetic, human touch.

On the other hand, when you're sharing something that's data driven or technical, or will need to be consulted in the future, opt for a detailed email, report, or memo that allows people to digest the information at their own pace. Formal proposals, especially those requiring approval from higher-ups, clients, or vendors, are usually best presented in a well-structured document or polished presentation versus a "back of the napkin" sketch. Similarly, if your idea affects a large group, opt for something scalable, like hosting a town hall, sending out a department-wide email, or recording a webinar, instead of relying solely on word of mouth.

What to Do When . . .

You Face Resistance

While some industries race into the future at breakneck speed, others, like government, legal services, and education, seem proudly tied to decades-old ways of doing things. The reasons for the disparity are complex and difficult to untangle, but they often stem from tradition, concerns about costs, and a culture of "that's not how we do things around here." That said, it's still possible to assume ownership, even in the face of resistance.

- **Utilize the door-in-the-face technique.** It's counterintuitive, but in situations where you anticipate an outright rejection, first propose a larger, more ambitious request. After it's shot down, ask for something more reasonable. Say your request to host a three-day offsite is rejected; you'd follow that up by asking, "How about we organize a half-day team-building event instead?"

- **Encourage debate and dissent**. People often resist change because they fear the unknown or the potential implications for their work. Rather than seeing this as a negative, reframe their reaction as a sign that they're invested. Perhaps you hold a "worst possible idea" brainstorm session or do a role-reversal debate where your peers argue for a position they disagree with. Creating space for people to voice their concerns and objections actually generates greater unity and morale.

- **Win over resistors**. Ask to team up, highlighting the importance of going further together with phrases like "I know when we both bring our strengths and ideas to the table, we'll achieve even better results" or "I think our complementary skills make us a powerful team. Could we partner on this project?"

- **Push the issue.** If your boss consistently ignores or overlooks your suggestions, get topics back on the table: "We haven't chatted about X in a while, but it's still on my mind. When can we check in?" Be candid about the impact or cost of not taking action, then ask for advice: "I've completed all the steps we talked about, but there have been no further developments, which has led to Y consequences. What would you do if you were me in this situation?"

- **Put jealousy in perspective.** When someone feels threatened by your ambition, recognize that envy is a reflection of their underrecognized desires or needs rather than a reflection of you. You shouldn't dim your success to make another person more comfortable, but it doesn't hurt to disarm them with honest compliments every once in a

while: "I really value your thoughts about this campaign"
or "I appreciated your take on delivery methods. It
changed my thinking."

You're the New Kid

If you've worked at one company or in one industry for a while, the
pathway to taking ownership may be easier or more obvious because you understand the landscape or have credibility to fall back
on. But what about when you're early in your career or new at your
company? In addition to using all the strategies in this chapter so
far, here's what else to do when you lack tenure or sit lower on the
chain of command:

- **Hold your horses.** Jumping straight into suggestion mode
  can alienate others, so take time to discern how decisions
  are made. Do things happen quickly based on one or two
  opinions, or is there lengthy deliberation involving many
  stakeholders? Are changes mostly safe, incremental
  improvements or major bold moves? When leadership
  uses words like "agility" and "disruption," it can suggest
  that assertively presenting your ideas is welcomed,
  whereas terms like "stability" and "caution" may mean
  you have to be more patient and thorough in your
  approach.

- **Know your place.** Every role serves one of five business
  needs: innovation (creating new services, R&D),
  maintenance (optimizing existing systems, focusing on
  efficiency), growth (scaling, increasing reach), support
  (facilitating the role of other departments), or compliance

(adherence to laws and regulations). By identifying your role's purpose, you can gauge the appropriate level and pace of change to advocate for. Alberto, a new test prep curriculum developer, had been hired for a maintenance role (streamlining the company's existing question database), but upon starting his job, he immediately saw that their teaching methods needed a complete overhaul (innovation). Rather than appear overzealous, he began adding supplementary quizzes and flash cards to gradually introduce new learning approaches.

- **Get a few wins under your belt.** In the early stages of your career or a new job, you're essentially an unknown quantity. Aim for one to two successes within the first three to six months to quickly establish your presence and credibility. Your opinions and suggestions will carry more weight, and you're more likely to be given the latitude to work independently. Choose projects that will be visible to key players and that have a clear, measurable impact.

- **Probe gently.** Using appreciative inquiry (i.e., using a strengths-based versus problem-based framing) can be a clever way to uncover what's working well *and* what's lacking. For example, when you say, "It seems like our client onboarding process is smooth when we do X. What makes X so successful compared to other parts of the process?," your boss or colleagues may then inadvertently point out shortcomings, giving you a natural opening to later propose a better way.

- **Use "we" and "I wonder."** Shifting to the royal "we" is one way to position yourself as of a higher status, and invoking

wonder can make others more open to discussing and
entertaining your ideas because you're presenting them in
a nonthreatening, exploratory manner. For instance, "Let's
acknowledge the incredible work everyone has put into
[current process]. It's clear a lot of effort and thought has
gone into this, and it's been a huge part of [positive
outcome]. I was wondering if we could consider [your
idea] as a way to build on what we're already doing. It
might help us with [specific challenge or opportunity],
adding to the strong foundation already in place."

You Royally Screw Up

Sometimes the ownership conversation means taking responsibility for overstepping or making mistakes. Early in my career, I
worked in a research lab and accidentally deleted an entire folder of
data that had taken months (and thousands of dollars) to gather.
At the time, I didn't know how to handle it, so I decided not to
handle it at all. I quit the job several weeks later. You can do
better—and the fact is, you'll *have to*. Here's how:

- **Assess the damage.** A rushed solution can sometimes lead
  to more problems. Take a moment to assess: Who's been
  impacted, and what's the potential consequence? You
  don't need to call attention to every tiny misstep you
  make, but in cases where there is reputational risk, loss
  to the company, or other high stakes, then the more
  information you have, the better.

- **Never let others be caught off guard.** When Natalie, an
  operations executive, was accused of unfairly kicking

someone off a project (after repeated warnings about his poor performance), she swallowed her pride and told her boss about what had happened and about the upcoming HR investigation, explaining that she had extensive documentation and would fully cooperate. Her boss was frustrated because this wasn't a slowdown that Natalie or the team needed, but he wasn't concerned about the situation blowing up further because Natalie had things under control. Sharing this bad news with her boss let Natalie shape his perception and eased his concerns, placing her at an advantage.

- **Don't soften the blow.** Apologize genuinely and straightforwardly: "I'm sorry I dropped the ball" or "I apologize for not meeting expectations." People tend to be more forgiving when they see the person behind the action, not just the mistake itself. Try phrasing like "I've heard concerns about [specific action]. My intent was [explanation], but I now see that there were unintended consequences" or "This experience has been a learning curve for me. My aim was [intention], but I understand the execution was off."

- **Make your actions speak louder.** Instead of continuing to bring up again and again how sorry you are, show it. Fix the error if it's within your expertise and purview to do so. Need outside assistance? Speak to your boss and get on the same page about next steps so you can present a plan to those in power. Turn your misstep or overreach into a systemic improvement. Maybe clearer communication channels are required or perhaps better criteria for vetting options need to be developed.

- **Take time out.** If there's an opportunity to work on a different project or collaborate with a different team for a while, consider it. This isn't about running away, but about giving space for emotions to settle. When you do reengage, it can be with a cleaner slate.

Sure, the ownership conversation can result in obvious rewards like promotions, raises, and a better seat at the table. What's even sweeter are the subtle benefits, like greater respect from your colleagues, as well as the satisfaction you feel when you see a project through to completion. Like Seiko, we all have barriers at work that we live with as routine annoyances (or worse!), but we don't have to. Write down the top three frustrations that keep you and your colleagues from operating as efficiently as you might like, then look at the list at the start of this chapter and determine if any one of them is ripe for taking initiative to solve.

While the thrill of leading a project and earning accolades is undeniable, beware of projects that turn into energy drains with little to no upside. Look for signs like continuously shifting goals, diminishing returns on your time, or escalating frustrations without resolution. Cutting your losses on a project that's going nowhere is a smart choice, not a sign of defeat. In your quest for ownership, also be mindful not to unintentionally take on *too* much. Up next in the boundaries conversation, you'll learn how to say no when it really counts.

CHAPTER FOUR

The Boundaries Conversation

Say no and set limits without being a complete jerk

Drew, a research manager at a city environmental agency, was getting ready to draft his resignation letter. He and his colleagues had just accomplished one of their major goals—a multi-year site cleanup, which involved rehabilitating a former block of condemned buildings into senior living with an attached community center. But rather than celebrate their hard work, his boss, Melina, had almost immediately launched into their next project and was insisting he conduct preliminary studies within the month.

While Drew felt his career was a calling and that he was doing his part to improve the city he had grown up in, the pace at which

Melina expected him to work was unsustainable. Drew was happy to put in extra hours to meet key deadlines, but Melina viewed every project as critical. He worried about the consequences if he failed to oblige her, and he couldn't help but be nervous about a bad performance review or even retaliation from Melina or others if he didn't keep up with the near-constant sprint. Objectively, his career was thriving—he was exceeding benchmarks and his team had grown by 50 percent since he started at the agency—but he was seriously considering quitting, just so he could get some peace.

"And then I came into the office on Tuesday, and Melina had moved up the study deadline by a week so that she could present the results to *her* boss," Drew explained in our coaching session. "She made a snide remark about how she'd be working the next few Saturdays. After finishing up a two-month sprint on another project, I'm *exhausted*. But she keeps speeding up and giving me more and more assignments on aggressive timelines. I guess I just need to decide to work harder or move on." He shrugged.

"Or maybe it's not about doing more this time," I said. "Maybe it's about finally setting some limits."

Even though he was concerned about making waves, Drew mustered the courage to ping Melina for a quick chat. "Finishing the site cleanup was really important for us and the agency, and I did everything I could to make it successful," he began, "but I'd like to reset expectations around timelines. What's driving the urgency around this latest project? I ask because I can't deliver the results you're used to if we're in a constant sprint, and I don't think it's re-alistic to ask the team to meet short deadlines or give up their weekends without a meaningful reason."

Melina grimaced, groaned, and huffed. "Well, this client is important . . . and we're all working hard around here . . . and . . . I don't know . . . let me think about it." She rushed off and avoided

Drew for the rest of the day. He was sure he was going to get fired. But the next morning, much to his surprise, Melina appeared at his office door. "So I thought about what you said. While I don't agree the current deadline is unreasonable, I also can't afford to have you or anyone else burning out," she explained. "So what do you think is a fair turnaround time as far as getting the preliminary studies done?" With that one decision to set limits diplomatically, Drew opened up the opportunity to move forward in a more thoughtful, deliberate way, which proved to be a better strategy than leaving or giving in to all of Melina's demands.

While standing up to your boss may feel nerve-racking, sometimes there's no other choice if you want to protect your time and energy in a way that preserves—even *grows*—the level of respect and credibility you command. That's why *the boundaries conversation*, which involves navigating the tricky nuances of tactfully saying no and setting limits at work without alienating others, is so critical. It's human nature to want to be agreeable and to worry about coming across as difficult or overstepping, but failing to say something can ultimately do more harm than good. Research finds that employees who chronically go beyond the call of duty not only have higher levels of job stress, role overload, and work-family conflict, but also feel more worn-out, tired, and on edge, what researchers call "organizational citizenship fatigue."

You may be surprised to learn that many people seek out coaching with me after being denied a promotion as a result of being told that they say yes to everything and don't know how to prioritize. Up until then, it's never occurred to them that a little diplomatic resistance might actually demonstrate that they have sound judgment and a willingness to have hard conversations. But while no might be a complete sentence in other areas of life, things aren't so simple at work, so in this chapter we'll demystify the emotionally

charged and complex social dynamics involved with asserting yourself. You'll learn how to gauge how hard you can push back and
how to balance standing your ground with being seen as a team
player. And because there's always a chance you'll rub someone the
wrong way, we'll also cover what to do when saying no sparks back-
lash. By mastering the boundaries conversation, you can approach
each day with a clear mind, ready to tackle important challenges
head-on rather than frantically juggling a never-ending to-do list.
It opens up the space for you to do work that's both fulfilling and
impactful, letting you leave the office with enough energy to enjoy
life outside of it.

Pick Your Battles

Boundaries at work encompass everything from how close someone stands to you or whether you drink alcohol at company parties
to how much your identity stems from interests and activities other
than your job. We'll touch on different forms of boundaries throughout the rest of this book, but for the purposes of this chapter, we'll
focus on two specific types: time and tasks. These are at the source
of the majority of work-life conflicts, where demands from your
boss or others often require saying no most frequently. Here are
some examples:

Extra assignments

- Deflecting administrative or non-promotable tasks (i.e.,
  work that isn't visible, doesn't require special skills, or
  doesn't add to the company's most important goals like

taking notes, scheduling meetings, or handling low-revenue clients)

- Turning down additional responsibilities when you're already leading multiple high-priority projects

- Not taking on a project that has been passed down from someone else who consistently avoids their responsibilities

Extended work hours

- Refusing an expectation to respond to emails late at night or on weekends when it's not an emergency

- Resisting external pressure to shorten your lunch break or other rest periods to meet demands

- Declining a request that would require working during your long-planned vacation

Unrealistic deadlines

- Objecting to a tight turnaround time on something that is highly complex or that requires lots of research or input from different people

- Saying no to a last-minute request that conflicts with a personal commitment you've shared in advance

- Rejecting a request to cover for a colleague's responsibilities without prior notice or adequate transition time

More meetings

- Declining meetings scheduled during your designated deep-work or creative time

- Excusing yourself from invitations to optional or nonessential calls that don't require your expertise or contribution

- Curbing frequent ad hoc drop-ins that interrupt your concentration

You can't say no to everything at work, so figuring out where you want to selectively stand your ground is key. But you might not know where to start with setting limits or how assertive you can be. One useful strategy is to keep a boundary inventory for a week. Specifically, document results from "the four feelings test," which I shared in my first book, *Trust Yourself.* Put simply, whenever you feel resentment, frustration, tension, or discomfort at work, make a note of the situation. What was asked of you? Why did it make you feel that way? What did you wish you could have said or done differently? Review your notes at the end of the week and look for patterns. Ask yourself the following questions and choose one boundary from your journal to focus on for the rest of this chapter:

1. **How is this situation affecting my well-being, productivity, or job satisfaction?** The more it negatively impacts you, the more pressing it is to speak up.

2. **Is this a one-time occurrence or a chronic issue?** A persistent problem will continue to eat away at you unless it's addressed.

3. **Is the boundary enforceable given my current role and responsibilities?** Maybe you can't say no to a project that comes from the CEO, but you can work with your manager to reprioritize everything else on your plate.

4. **How disruptive will my request be?** You'll face less resistance if you prioritize situations that only affect you and your work and not your entire team.

5. **Can I articulate why this limit is important to me—and beneficial to others?** Boundaries that protect your most important values and priorities should be at the top of your list—and having a clear reasoning makes it easier for others to respect your point of view.

6. **What's the cost of *not* setting this boundary?** If you continue working late, for example, consider the impact on your personal life. Are you okay with that sacrifice?

Deliver a Nuanced No

Beyond assessing when you *should* say no, you also have to consider whether you *can* say no. This means assessing your pushback power: the leverage you have to decline, your boss's openness to boundaries, and how your request might be seen by others. If your pushback power is lower, you'll need to take a softer, more cautious approach to setting limits. But if your pushback power is higher, you can be more direct about your needs.

	↓ Lower Pushback Power	↑ Higher Pushback Power
Your tenure and position	— You hold an entry-level or junior role, which means your opinions carry less sway. — You've been at the company for one year or less or have moved between different roles and departments a lot. — Your role is less structured, which means you may be expected to "pinch-hit" and take on many different responsibilities.	+ You hold a senior or leadership role, which naturally comes with more influence and authority. + You have a long tenure with the organization or have been promoted a few times, so you "get" the company's culture and are seen as a key player. + You have specialized knowledge, so the company is more likely to accommodate your needs to retain you.
Your relationship with your boss	— You have minimal interaction with your boss—maybe only during formal meetings—which makes it hard to build rapport and trust. — Communication feels one-sided, with little room for your input or concerns, lowering your influence. — Your boss doesn't actively support your professional growth or career development, suggesting they may not see your long-term potential.	+ Your boss often seeks your advice and input on important decisions, showing that they value your judgment. + Your boss consistently supports your ideas and initiatives, suggesting they trust your capabilities. + There's mutual respect between you and your manager because you can respectfully disagree and solve problems together.

	⬇ Lower Pushback Power	⬆ Higher Pushback Power
Your boss's management style	— Even when colleagues show clear signs of burnout like lower productivity, your boss brushes over the issue and doesn't offer help. — When team members voice concerns about workload or stress, your boss dismisses them or tells them to "just push through." — Your boss constantly shifts expectations or feels the need to control every detail, making it harder to gain autonomy.	+ Your boss is generally attuned to the team's bandwidth and morale and proactively supports team members who seem overwhelmed. + Your boss has a history of setting clear expectations and reevaluating them frequently, showing they might be more open to making adjustments. + You and your boss have regular touchpoints where you discuss your challenges, giving you a platform to bring up requests.
The organizational culture and context	— The company often reacts to crises and short-term needs, prioritizing immediate fixes over long-term planning and sustainability. — The organization is going through a period of high stress or financial strain, placing a heavy focus on output and lowering people's openness to change. — There are strict policies with little room for exceptions or adjustments, making it difficult to negotiate special requests.	+ Other employees have successfully negotiated for flexible work arrangements, extra time off, or scaled-back workloads. + Leadership talks about the importance of work-life balance and openly supports employee well-being. + The company has channels for feedback, whether surveys, town halls, or open-door policies, that encourage employees to voice their concerns and suggestions.

Not every category will always be in your favor, and that's okay. Plus, you probably have more leverage than you think. Managers want to retain good people. Turnover costs more than $1 trillion a year and takes a ton of time. Even if your manager seems resistant to your requests, keeping you makes their life easier than trying to hire someone new, and their success (including promotions and bonuses) often depends on having a stable, productive team.

By having the boundaries conversation, you're standing up for yourself and, over the long term, making sure you can give high-quality effort and bring smart ideas to your team. Just because you're a salaried employee doesn't mean you have to work endless hours. That's neither healthy for you nor productive for the company in the long run! Your results matter more than just having your butt in a chair, but it's up to you to make this case compellingly, which is why in a moment we'll get into how to frame your boundaries around how they benefit your boss and the business.

Dig for Details

No matter your level of pushback power, saying no without a second thought might not always serve *your* best interests. That's why before you say no, it's important to ask your manager one or more of the following questions to understand what's truly involved:

- **For extra assignments, try:** Is there a particular reason you thought of me for this task? How does this task support our goals? Given my current workload, how do you see this new assignment fitting in? Is this a short-term need or something you see becoming a regular part of my role?

- **For extended work hours, try:** Please help me understand the urgency behind these after-hours requests—are there specific deadlines we're trying to meet? Can we set clear guidelines for what warrants a fast reply? I want to understand the impact better—are there consequences to waiting to tackle this within standard hours? In terms of skipping lunch, can we identify specific outcomes we're aiming for with this extra effort?

- **For unrealistic deadlines, try:** What specific factors determined this turnaround time? Are there milestones or external pressures driving the tight due date? Can we revisit expectations in light of the project's scope and complexity? What flexibility is there to adjust the deliverables or resources for this assignment?

- **For more meetings, try:** Before we jump on a call, could you send over your specific questions first? I may be able to answer most via email. Could you share the agenda for the meeting this week? Knowing who's attending and what decisions need to be made will help me determine if my presence will be helpful. Is there an option to get a summary or action items post-discussion? It makes more sense to have [team member] attend since they're closer to this project—is that good for you?

By asking smart questions, you can evaluate the potential return on investment of your time and effort. Is an extra assignment an opportunity to showcase your abilities to senior management? Does stepping in to give a second opinion about how to move forward actually offer a chance to influence a critical project? You may also uncover details that allow you to negotiate or decline requests more easily. If it becomes clear that your input isn't essential for a meeting, for instance, you've found a strong justification to excuse yourself. Plus, asking questions subtly challenges the other party to justify their request as well. Through talking with you, your manager may come to the realization on their own that it makes more sense to delegate a task to your colleague or to automate it to save time and resources.

Make Strategic Concessions

Let's say your boss asks you to turn around presentation slides from scratch in twenty-four hours on top of your existing workload. Agreeing might feel like self-betrayal, but consider the bigger picture: You're building professional equity and investing in the relationship. Plus, you're sending the message that you'll be there when it counts, which earns you goodwill.

Steal these scripts to agree without being a pushover or, worse, suggesting you're just doing your boss a favor:

The conditional yes

When your pushback power is on the lower side, consider obliging the request once or twice, ensuring it's recognized as an exception.

- I understand how crucial this project is and I'm ready to take it on this time, but I want to make sure we both know that I can't always accommodate last-minute changes.

- I'm on board to help with this because I know it's urgent. I do hope, though, that we can view this as a special case.

- I'll stay late to tackle this [task] because I know it's important, but I'd appreciate it if we could consider this an exception rather than the norm.

- I'm willing to be available during my time off for this particular project. Once I'm back, let's talk about how we can handle similar situations in the future.

The trade-off

Put the decision-making back in your manager's hands to respect their authority and turn a potential conflict into a priority-setting exercise.

- I'm focused on getting X done by the deadline we agreed on. Adding Y would impact that timeline. How should we reprioritize?

- If I extend my work hours this week for X, what tasks would you like me to push out to next week to compensate?

- Meeting this deadline means deprioritizing something else temporarily. What would you prefer we slow down on?

- To make room for these meetings, I need to delegate some of my current tasks. Which do you recommend I hand off?

The deferral

From a psychological standpoint, creating space between the request and your acceptance puts you in a position of control and shows you're conscientious.

- Can we review this tomorrow? I need to look at my calendar and see what I can adjust.

- Before I commit to another meeting, let me review my current project timelines. I'll follow up with you.

- This deadline seems tight. Can I review our resources and timelines and suggest a more feasible date?

- I appreciate your thinking of me for this. Let me assess my current workload and see where this might fit.

The referral

In some cases, you might have the opportunity to direct your boss to someone else.

- For [after-hours task], I might not be the fastest. [Colleague] would be more responsive. Want me to check if they can step in?

- I can't make this meeting due to a conflict, but [colleague] has been closely involved and can represent our team well.

- I'm stretched thin with current projects. [Colleague] has a similar skill set and might have the bandwidth to take this on. Should I see if they're available?

- Considering the deadline, I might not be the best choice. [Colleague] has done similar work in shorter times. How about them?

Resetting expectations after you make concessions is key, and when you're ready, you can do so from a stronger position. Try your best to connect the reset to any past agreements you've established, say through the styles conversation. Using the observations you've made about your boss's style from chapter 2, you can frame the benefits around what they care about the most:

- **With a Commander boss, emphasize efficiency and achievement.** If declining extra tasks, explain how focusing on your core responsibilities translates to faster completion of high-priority projects.

- **With a Cheerleader boss, focus on image and long-term impact.** Here's how to say no to a meeting: "I think focusing on [project] will have a greater impact on our reputation for innovation than attending another meeting."

- **With a Caretaker boss, stress well-being and stability.** If pushing back on extended work hours, explain how balancing work and personal time improves your overall health and keeps you motivated, which is in everyone's best interest.

- **With a Controller boss, highlight precision and quality.** If you're pushing back on an unrealistic deadline, make the case for how a slightly extended timeline would allow for more thorough research and ultimately a more accurate result.

Pay attention to how your colleagues present boundaries to your boss, too. Say you've noticed that one of your teammates, Erica, seems to have a knack for pushing back on unreasonable requests from your shared manager. The next time you see Erica do this in a meeting, make a mental note of her language and tone—and maybe even follow up with her afterward to learn more. Erica might share that she's found it effective to frame her boundaries in terms of business outcomes (e.g., "If I take on this new project, it will delay the launch of X by two weeks") or to offer alternative solutions (e.g., "I can take on A if we can bring in some additional support for B").

Sell It on the Spot

Even after you've reset expectations, sooner or later your boss will test the waters again. This doesn't necessarily mean they don't respect you. It's more a facet of their role: Everyone at every level is under pressure to get more done and that trickles down to you. While you can't guarantee that anyone, especially your manager, will accept your boundaries every time, you can significantly increase the chances that they'll be receptive by using some savvy persuasion skills and being prepared to assertively reaffirm your limits.

Sharing insight into your workload or the dilemma you're facing can trigger empathy and mutual understanding from your manager, but keep it concise. Overexplaining can make you sound insecure and open you up to objection handling, when others try to poke holes in your reasoning or persuade you, so try scripts like these instead:

- I want to give you some context on why I'm hesitant to say yes to this [new assignment]. This month, I've already committed to [projects/tasks]. Adding something else to my workload may squeeze out time needed for these deliverables.

- Late nights are starting to take their toll on my focus and productivity. Could we identify the must-respond messages I have to get to today and what can be punted to next week?

- Given the complexity of [task] and the importance of getting it right, I'm concerned that the current deadline is too ambitious. I want to be realistic about what can be achieved in the given time frame and ensure that we set ourselves up for success, not failure. I'd suggest we [proposal], which will balance speed and quality.

Your boss, like everyone, is tuned in to their personal "radio station," WII-FM (What's In It For Me?). Broadcast on their frequency, emphasizing how the boundary you're setting not only meets *your* needs but also aligns with *their* priorities (and pressures) and serves the greater good. By connecting how your saying no can lead to better, higher-quality work, more creative solutions, or a more engaged and less burned-out team, you appeal to your manager's interest and make it easier for them to see the value in accepting your pushback.

Navigate Pushback to Your Pushback

You can't ever know for sure how someone will react when you say no, but looking back at the criteria under the "Deliver a Nuanced No" section can help you anticipate your manager's possible response. For instance, if you've built strong rapport, your boss may be more understanding when you try to decline extra tasks. On the other hand, when they're under a lot of stress or facing pressure from their own management, even the kindest boss may not like it if you refuse to cover a few meetings for them. Likewise, the broader organizational culture—whether it encourages open dialogue or prefers conformity, for example—also plays a role.

Regardless of how tactfully you deliver your boundary, it's important to prepare for a less than positive reaction and be ready to navigate the situation constructively. Below I've suggested several scripts for the most common scenarios from the least to most assertive:

Frustration

What it sounds like: Wow, I have to say that I'm disappointed. I was counting on you to handle this. This puts me in a really bad spot.
How to respond: Offer what you *can* do to show you're collaborative and proactively searching for solutions.

- I know this is a busy time for the team, and I want to do my part. I have a hard stop at six o'clock today for a family commitment. Would it be possible for me to come in early tomorrow instead to wrap up the deliverables?

- I understand this puts you in a difficult position, and that's not my intent. I want to be as supportive as possible. Since I can't lead this new project with everything else I have on my plate, I could consult or help with [specific aspect]. How does that sound?

- I know it's important someone represents us on [project]. Maybe we could find a middle ground? I can't make weekly meetings work, but a call every two weeks could be a good solution.

- I completely understand that this is urgent. At the same time, it's not doable to have the entire report done by Friday. What if I get you the first section by then? I can prioritize finishing the rest early next week.

Guilt-tripping

What it sounds like: I thought you were a team player. This makes me question how badly you really want to succeed here. It doesn't seem like you're as dedicated as I thought.

How to respond: Challenge your boss's assumption while highlighting why your boundary is in their best interest.

- You're right—I do care about being a team player and I want to be as productive as possible for everyone's benefit. So, do you think we could combine meetings that cover similar topics? Then I could refocus my time on higher-value tasks.

- One of my top priorities is to make you and the team successful. The best way I can do that is by taking care of myself so I can pitch in fully and not leave others to pick up my slack. Could we revisit how we're balancing my workload so I don't burn out?

- It's the opposite actually. I'm invested in us doing well, which is why I'm suggesting that we adjust the deadline just slightly so we're realistic about what we can accomplish.

- To really hit our goals, I need to focus on the areas where I can make the biggest impact, which we've agreed is X. So, can we talk about how I can say no to Y?

Minimizing

What it sounds like: Try to organize your time better, or maybe skip your kids' soccer game just this once. If you work a bit faster, you can fit this in no problem.

How to respond: Acknowledge your manager's suggestions while clarifying the limitations and potential negative side effects of their proposed shortcuts.

- I appreciate you trying to help me find a way to fit this in. The thing is, my schedule is already pretty packed, and shifting things around doesn't quite solve the overall workload issue. Do you think we could explore another way to handle this?

- I hear your advice about working faster, and I'll do my best. But I'm worried that rushing might lead to mistakes. Maybe we can prioritize which parts of the project need immediate attention?

- Thanks for the suggestion, but working through my breaks each week might not be the best long-term solution. Instead, I'm hoping I could [your solution]. What do you think?

- I get that you want this done quickly, and I appreciate your input. Just squeezing this in isn't as simple as it sounds and skipping my personal commitment isn't something I'm comfortable with. I'd prefer it if we could look at other options.

Comparison

What it sounds like: LeAnn stays late every day and hasn't complained. Burnham juggles twice as many tasks as this, so I don't understand why you're struggling.

How to respond: Bring the conversation back to your own circumstances without undermining your colleagues.

- I understand that the team is under a lot of pressure, and I want to make sure I'm doing my part. For me, that means balancing my workload so I can meet our clients' expectations. Would you mind helping me figure out a more manageable way to structure the tasks on my plate right now?

- I completely respect how everyone brings something different to the table. Since we all also have different responsibilities outside of work, maybe we could discuss what tasks would be feasible for me to manage within regular hours?

- I see your point, but my focused work happens best during my heads-down time. Can we find another time for the meeting?

- Setting aside [colleague's] situation, let's get back to discussing what would be a reasonable turnaround time for X. I think that would be a better use of time.

Beyond the Conversation

Avoid Undermining Yourself

Sometimes jitters can cause you to unintentionally weaken your stance at the outset of the conversation. This can include apologizing excessively (e.g., "I'm so sorry" or "I feel bad bringing this up"), using tentative language (e.g., "I guess it's not a big deal" or "I don't mean to be a pain"), overqualifying with too many details (e.g., "I have projects X and Y on my plate. My kids are sick and we have family coming in next week. On top of all that, I also . . ."). It's totally normal to feel nervous when setting a boundary, but even if you're freaking out on the inside, you can still appear composed on the outside.

Take Simone, a junior content writer. When pushing back on unrealistic deadlines from her manager, she often softened her delivery with phrases like "I hope you won't be mad" and "I hate to do this . . ." Simone thought she was being polite, but her boss didn't see her limits as serious. "We all have to stretch ourselves sometimes," he said and brushed Simone's concerns aside.

Simone decided it was time to change her approach. She started by speaking more slowly, which gave her time to think and ensured she wasn't defaulting to qualifiers that undermined her. She swapped apology for gratitude. Instead of "I'm so sorry I can't accommodate this," she'd say, "Thanks for thinking of me. I'm glad I came to mind for this task." After delivering her boundary, Simone allowed her boss to consider her words before jumping in to fill the space with unnecessary backtracking like "Don't worry—if speaking with the client is an issue, then I'll just find the time to handle this." To keep her new approach top of mind, she placed a sticky note on her monitor that read "It's selfish not to say no" and "Boundaries help you say yes to what serves you" as a constant visual cue to reassess her instinct to undermine herself.

When Simone began delivering her no with greater confidence, her manager's response shifted as well. He began considering her viewpoint rather than immediately dismissing it. The change wasn't instant or perfect, but Simone noticed that her firmer, more self-assured approach led to a noticeable improvement in how her boundaries were received and respected.

Streamline Your Time

The boundaries conversation extends to pushback with your colleagues, too. After all, the way you set limits with peers directly impacts your mental, emotional, and literal capacity to handle requests from superiors (which are usually more important). Since you and your peers typically share an equal level of power, you can be more direct. For example, at the top of a meeting, as you're discussing projects, let your colleagues know that you won't be able to fit anything new into your schedule for the next two weeks because of another pressing matter. Or, if a team member calls you up out of the blue to chat, begin by saying you only have ten minutes to talk or that you have a hard stop at the top of the hour.

To minimize interruptions from colleagues who frequently stop by for chats or impromptu meetings, consider establishing "office hours"—designated blocks where others can book a slot or simply drop in for questions. You can also create processes that streamline random and time-consuming requests. Ed, a product manager at a consumer goods company, found himself constantly triaging demands from business development, marketing, and sales. Instead of taking on the many to-dos his cross-functional partners threw at him in emails or via Slack, he started a company wiki where he invited his colleagues to post questions that he answered for ninety minutes once a week. He also requested that they do a simple search before posting to confirm that the question hadn't already been answered. At first, people didn't oblige, but after he stopped reanswering questions and started pointing people toward previous responses, they got the message. This simple step forced the other teams to be more intentional and detailed about what they were asking for, which significantly cut down on the number of requests he received.

Even if you don't feel you have the authority to set up new systems or make meaningful changes, you can still streamline your time by getting your manager's blessing. Try asking something like "After we identify which meetings I can step back from, can I count on your support if there are any questions or concerns from others about my absence? Having your endorsement will make this transition smoother for everyone." You could also say, "I've noticed that managing ad hoc requests and interruptions has been impacting my ability to focus on our top priorities. With your approval, I'd like to [streamlining suggestion]. I want to make sure I have your backing before I move forward."

What to Do When . . .

Your Manager Refuses to Be Refused

You might try every tactic in the earlier section on navigating pushback to your pushback and *still* find your boss bulldozing your boundaries. While some managers are open to negotiating a middle ground that works for you, them, and the company, others won't take no for an answer. Try the following tactics when your boss relentlessly disregards your needs and insists on having their way:

- **Lighten the mood.** A touch of wit can diffuse tension and remind your boss of your shared humanity, but be careful not to be sarcastic or offensive. Try something like "If only my day had twenty-five hours, then maybe I could fit this in, but for now we'll have to work with the bandwidth I have" or "I'd love to clone myself, but since that's not an option, let's talk about what's realistic."

- **Be a broken record.** Calmly restate your stance with phrases like "As we discussed before, I can't take this on due to my current workload. I hope we can both agree to honor that," "Again, that's not something I can commit to, and I'd appreciate you respecting that," or "I have to be clear: Working over the weekend is not an option. I'm confident we can find another way to get those assignments done."

- **Don't give in to tit for tat.** A bullying boss may raise their voice or speed up their speech to assert dominance, unsettle you, and get you to capitulate under pressure. Whatever you do, don't mirror this behavior. Matching their aggression only escalates the situation. Regulate yourself with grounding practices—take five deep belly breaths, relax your hips into your chair, or hold on to a pen in your hands to redirect your nervous energy.

- **Shield yourself.** Many of my coaching clients find it helpful to visualize a glass pane between them and the other person—a reminder not to take on and internalize another's anger. Consider how someone you admire would handle the situation. Channeling your hero can

put you in a stronger position to put your best foot
forward.

- **Allow for dead air.** Sometimes the most powerful thing
  you can do is say nothing at all. Gloria, a veterinary
  tech, told me, "My manager wasn't listening to reason,
  but instead of agreeing or filling the space by
  acquiescing, I waited five to ten seconds after everything
  she said. She ended up filling in that empty space with
  more options and even included the route I proposed to
  them after all."

You Work in an "Always-On" Company or Industry

Maybe you're in an industry like advertising, entertainment, or consulting, where the expectation is that you respond to messages seconds after they're received. Or perhaps you've found that others
book over your lunch hour or do-not-disturb times without a second thought. You can't magically change the culture, but you can
use these tips to thrive within it:

- **Acknowledge receipt.** Reassure the sender that you've seen
  their message, even if you can't reply in detail right away.
  Responses like "Received, thank you" or "Noted, I'll
  tackle this first thing tomorrow" go a long way to
  showing people you're attentive and responsive, while
  also allowing you to get to things on your schedule.

- **Step up your status updates.** Swap generic status indicators
  like "Available" or "Do Not Disturb" for customized
  statuses that provide more information. For example:
  "Lunch until 1pm," "Offline for the day—will check

messages at 8am tomorrow," or "Compiling the January numbers." Colleagues can then adjust their expectations accordingly and are more likely to respect your boundaries when they understand what you're working on and when you'll be free.

- **Book buffer time.** When scheduling your workday or week, intentionally allocate only 80 percent of your available time to planned tasks, meetings, and projects. This leaves you with 20 percent of your time as a buffer that allows you to accommodate surprise interruptions and requests. You can also designate a thirty-to-sixty-minute block per day (ideally at a lower-energy time) or ten to fifteen minutes between meetings to handle unexpected issues or simply take short breaks to recharge.

- **Define what qualifies as an emergency.** During last year's summer vacation, Safiyah, a billing specialist, found herself inundated with "urgent" requests from her counterparts in accounting. So in advance of her next trip, she clarified what rose to the level of an emergency: "I'll be out from July 2 to 10. I won't be checking email, but you can text or call me if there's a significant billing error like a double charge, an issue processing payments, or if there's any suspicious activity on our accounts." You don't have to be out of the office to use this strategy; it works just as well to protect focused work time, your weekends, or even your lunch hour.

- **Set your own rules.** Choose designated times during the day when you'll respond to messages promptly and communicate these times to your team or put them in your email signature, especially if you work in an international organization, so everyone knows when to expect your replies. Set up a delay on your outgoing emails, making it appear as though you're not sending messages after hours.

Saying no may feel weird and awkward in the beginning, but what's worse? Navigating the short-term discomfort of advocating for yourself—or enduring weeks, months, or maybe even years of anxiety, anger, and resentment? Just imagine how much more enjoyable and comfortable work would be if you didn't have to stress over having extra work dumped on your plate. Or if you could effectively opt out when you're asked to attend that useless meeting *yet again*. How much space would asserting your needs and limits create to cultivate your interests and devote time to high-value work that brings you joy? Take a moment now to choose one boundary that would significantly impact your quality of life at work—and then communicate it to your manager using the strategies in this chapter. Not only will regularly thinking and talking about boundaries make your life better, but it's great practice for some of the other hard conversations we discuss in this book, like the feedback conversation, which we'll tackle next.

CHAPTER FIVE

The Feedback Conversation

Voice your opinion, even if you're afraid of pushback

No one is perfect, including your boss. While you may be able to live with some of their quirks, there will inevitably be times when you have to speak up for your own sake (and sanity) and that of your colleagues. Maybe your manager has canceled every one-on-one at the last minute for a month. Or perhaps they have a habit of making sarcastic comments about your work. Your boss might be quick to blame others or dominate conversations, leaving little room for outside input. Whatever the case, delivering constructive criticism up your chain of command can feel like walking a tightrope. You need to be persuasive enough to inspire your leader to change, yet diplomatic enough not to challenge their authority (or ego) in a way that backfires. Still, many worry that speaking up about anything at all will damage their relationship with their boss beyond repair. Others fear being branded a "troublemaker."

These concerns make sense, but they don't mean you're powerless. Let's say you're an employee relations specialist at a Fortune 100 company whose boss constantly shifts priorities. One week you're told to focus on resolving employee grievances, and the next you're pulled into designing company-wide training sessions. Because you spend so much time responding to new directives at the drop of a hat, you get overwhelmed and miss deadlines, which makes the team look bad. As a lower-ranking employee of a fifteen-member HR team, you convince yourself to "suck it up" and deal with your boss's behavior. But that only risks both *your* work life and the *team's* results getting worse. While you may be nervous about approaching your manager to describe how half-finished projects affect the team's reputation, it's critical to have that hard conversation. Because what I know now, after watching many of my clients suffer in silence, is that even if your boss doesn't immediately grasp the gravity of the situation, gently bringing up the issue can eventually pay off and pave the way for greater stability.

Of course, it's not as easy as it seems. While it would be nice to freely speak your mind at work anytime, the reality is more delicate. This chapter will give you specific criteria to help you decide if it's appropriate and worthwhile to provide input, along with guidelines for gauging the right timing to ensure your manager is receptive. I'll also show you a formula for delivering tough feedback that's focused on behavior—not personality—so you can address issues in a way that sets aside the personal and focuses on making meaningful changes that will positively affect you, your boss, your team, and often your entire workplace. Without a doubt, this requires tact and finesse—whether it's in a casual sidebar during the day or a formal, dedicated sit-down meeting—but many of my clients have navigated these tricky waters before, and you can, too.

While having *the feedback conversation* can bring you peace of mind, it's not a fix for every problem at work. At the end of the day, you can't control what your boss or anyone else does—or doesn't do—with the input you give, which my client Ramesh, a student program administrator, learned firsthand. Several weeks after the university he worked for undertook a search for a lead diversity officer, Ramesh went to the dean to deliver the committee's hiring recommendation. While this candidate, an accomplished Black woman, had been vetted by the entire committee and blew them away during interviews, the dean questioned whether her background was a good fit for the role.

"I could tell the dean was hesitating because this individual made him uncomfortable. She would challenge him, when what he wanted was a rule follower." Ramesh realized that he had to share his concerns. "If we don't hire this candidate," he told the dean, "we'll be showing our staff that we don't care about representation and that's going to lead to retention and morale issues." The dean didn't heed Ramesh's warning, and everyone on the committee resigned from their positions weeks later. "It's been a hot mess," Ramesh told me. "Even though it didn't work out as I hoped, I feel good about fighting for the change I believed would benefit everyone."

As Ramesh's story shows, even if you're unpleasantly surprised by your boss's reaction, it doesn't mean you'll regret saying your piece. That's why in this chapter, we'll also talk about how to stand your ground in the face of defensiveness, hostility, or total disregard. But know this: While it's true that not all managers welcome constructive criticism with open arms, I speak with executives all the time who desperately want to know how they can do their jobs better. In one survey, when asked if they would rather receive corrective feedback or praise, nearly 60 percent of respondents chose corrective feedback.

So remember, as uncomfortable as it may be to voice your opinion, speaking up can actually make your life better. Maybe you'll end up with clearer instructions and expectations, more respectful discussions, greater independence, or fewer frustrating last-minute changes and surprises. For your boss, your input can reveal blind spots they didn't know about and help them become a better leader. They may learn to manage their time better, delegate tasks more, keep their emotions in check, and communicate more transparently with the team. Whether your boss misses deadlines, is a chronic complainer, or has cut you out of one too many decisions, this chapter will show you how to shift from simply tolerating annoying habits and damaging behaviors to guiding your boss to treat you with the respect you deserve.

To Speak or Not to Speak? That Is the Question

How do you decide when to say something or whether to let it go? For example, maybe your boss has interrupted you during the last two team meetings. Do they not value your thoughts, or are they just enthusiastic? Or how about that time they corrected your work in front of senior management? Was it a misguided attempt at transparency or an effort to undermine you? Knowing when to say something isn't always clear-cut.

Before you decide to share a criticism, suggestion, or correction, ask yourself the following questions. If the answer to most of them is yes, then the situation probably warrants a conversation. If not, the costs of giving feedback might outweigh the potential benefits, or you may not have enough information to move forward yet. The only exception is when someone says something racist, bigoted, or offensive; in that case, you can and should make it clear straightaway that such behavior isn't acceptable (and we'll cover exactly how to do this later in this chapter, whether you're the target or an observer).

- **Has the situation or behavior in question happened before?** Say your manager asks for an hour-by-hour rundown of what you and your teammates are working on. If this happens once or twice, it could just mean that there's a project or situation that requires strict oversight—everyone oversteps at times—but if it becomes a consistent and stifling pattern over the course of weeks or months, address it.

- **Will there be consequences if I don't give this feedback soon?** A major monetary or business risk—losing an account, botching a release, potential poor media coverage—is always a reason to speak up. After a key sales meeting, Jackie overheard customers saying they were put off by her boss's hesitancy to commit to a course of action following a product recall. She decided to say something because failing to do so could have led to losing a million-dollar deal and tainted their reputation in the market.

- **Do I have all the facts?** Although Hector was upset by a major project delay, he paused before jumping to conclusions about the ineptitude of his boss, Rich. After looking more closely at emails and meeting notes, he uncovered a crucial detail: Senior management had instructed Rich to prioritize an urgent security update for their software, directly causing the delay in launching Hector's new feature. Your boss faces complexities and pressures you might not be aware of, and a decision that may seem questionable at first can be driven by unseen directives or stressors.

- **Am I prepared to be part of the solution?** Venting without ideas and suggestions about how to make things better is like shouting into a void—satisfying for a moment but ultimately useless. If your boss dismisses every suggestion you bring forward and you go to them griping, "You never listen to me!," it probably won't lead to change. Say instead, "I understand every idea can't be implemented, but I want to make sure mine are valuable. What criteria do you use to evaluate suggestions?"

- **Have I changed what I can control?** If you're silent in meetings, can you really blame your boss for not spotlighting your achievements? If your boss's instructions are vague and confusing, have you asked enough follow-up questions to get clarity? Before laying blame, ask yourself: Have I taken charge of what's within my power? Start by adjusting your own actions. This alone could change how your boss responds to you or eliminate the annoying behavior altogether.

PLAY THE WAITING GAME

You should always aim to deliver upward feedback privately, in real time (not via email or messaging, where nuance can be lost). But how long do you need to wait?

- **Immediate response (0–4 hours).** Anything that has major safety, legal, or financial ramifications—or that could cause a cascade of issues like customer complaints. For example, your boss sends out a promotional email with the wrong discount code or your skip-level misses an essential step or feature during a live product demo. It's more urgent, so there won't be time for a formal planned meeting. You're probably going to drop by your boss's desk or ping them on Messenger to ask if they have a second to chat.

- **Next business day (24–48 hours).** Most intense emotions, including irritation, last less than an hour. Say you're upset because your manager's public critique of your idea seemed to sabotage you, but you can't pinpoint the exact reasons why. Sleep on it and collect your thoughts so you can approach the conversation with a fresh—and more objective— perspective. Know your boss's style: If they prefer structure, schedule a meeting so they can mentally prepare: "Can we set aside some time tomorrow to chat about yesterday's launch? I'd like to go over a few points in detail." Otherwise, you can bring it up during a one-on-one or as an aside in another conversation: "I wanted to circle back to the comment you made yesterday . . ."

- **A week or longer.** For complex or sensitive matters, you'll need more time and space to gather data, speak to different people, and strategize an approach. For instance, you're aggravated by the fact that your boss seems to give your peer more leniency with deadlines. Instead of charging into his office, you observe how he handles holding other team members accountable to determine if this is a consistent issue. In almost all cases, you'll want to schedule a meeting in advance because your boss may have forgotten about the incident and moved on, so you'll need to jog their memory. They also might not realize that what you want to discuss is even an issue. Bringing this up can sound like: "I booked time for us on Monday since I'd like to get on the same page about how we're handling deadlines."

Adjust these timelines based on the severity of the issue, the personalities involved, and your organizational culture. And remember, timing and context are everything. Springing unexpected feedback on your leader right before a big team call or another high-pressure moment could derail them, which they could perceive as ill-informed and unsupportive. Plus, when key stakeholders (internal or external) are around, you, your colleagues, and your manager need to present a united front, or at least the appearance of one. Contradicting someone during a meeting with their superiors or clients could humiliate them, put them on the defensive, and ultimately weaken your own cause.

Craft a Constructive Critique

The best, most effective feedback tends to originate from slowing down, dissecting your frustrations, and getting specific about what you'd like to be different. By taking a pause, you gain perspective and make it more likely that you won't freeze up or get overly emotional in the moment. That space can also help ensure feedback is fair and not solely a product of your own anxiety (e.g., when you accuse your boss of slacking on email response times, but in fact you're just majorly stressed about a deadline).

Take a few minutes to jot down or mentally note any broad **assumptions** you're making about your boss's character or motivations. This gut reaction is for your eyes only—there to help you process your emotions, but not to share with your manager or anyone else. Then, define what this label actually looks like in action—the specific **behavior** you want to give feedback on. Finally, envision what a positive **change** would look like. For example:

Assumption	Behavior	Change
My boss is a micromanager.	My boss requires being cc'd on emails about minor office supply orders.	I'd like to agree on specific types of decisions or emails that require their input so I have more autonomy over my work.
My boss is flighty and all over the place.	My boss pivoted from project A to B without explanation.	Ask that shifts in focus are shared with a brief explanation of the reasons behind them to keep the team aligned.

Assumption	Behavior	Change
My boss is never there when I need them.	My boss regularly postpones our one-on-ones and doesn't respond to emails asking to reschedule.	During the weeks when we can't meet live, let's do a quick check-in via Messenger.
My boss always shifts the blame to me.	When a client complained about a missed deadline, my boss attributed the issue to me in front of senior management without acknowledging they took a month on the approvals.	In future situations, address any issues internally first to avoid any negative perceptions from the leadership team.
My boss acts like a dictator.	They decided on a new project management tool for the team without consulting us, even though it significantly alters our workflow.	I'd like to do a trial period for new tools where the team can provide feedback before a full rollout is green-lit.

Gather receipts—meeting minutes, performance metrics, survey results, change logs, and other forms of documentation—to transform "I feel like you do X" to "Here's what happened." If your boss switches priorities all the time, having emails in which other stakeholders or clients express confusion can speak volumes. If your boss blames you for a project falling behind, come prepared with a timeline that shows when you submitted your parts versus when you received their approvals. Hopefully you don't have to lay your evidence on the table, but it's a good idea to have it in your back pocket to lend weight to your words if needed.

Make It About Them (in a Good Way)

When the moment of truth arrives, use the specifics you've identified to ask a targeted question like "Do you have a few minutes to talk about our last conversation with the client?" or "Can I offer some input on how the project went?" This is less likely to trigger alarm bells and subtly secures a small moment of agreement from your boss. Getting this "micro-yes," a strategy rooted in the "mere agreement" principle, leads them to be more open to the conversation that follows.

When it comes to productive conflict, we're commonly told to focus on ourselves and our feelings, but for the feedback conversation, the exact opposite is true. Rather than leading with your own concerns and suggestions, put yourself in your boss's shoes first and try to imagine the situation from their point of view. This way you can create a shared goal based on what will resonate with your boss the most.

If you haven't had a chance to pinpoint your boss's exact style as described in chapter 2, that's okay. Take your best guess based on your interactions and observations so far. The goal here is to approach the conversation in a way that feels respectful and constructive to both of you:

- **With a Commander boss, try:** "I want us to be successful with [project], so I'd like to talk about some things that will help" or "I see an opportunity for us to achieve even more by reassessing how work gets evenly delegated."

Avoid emotional words in favor of results-oriented language.

- **With a Cheerleader boss, try:** "I'd like to clear something up with you because I think it'll make a big difference in how our efforts are received by [key stakeholder]" or "I've noticed I could use a bit more detail in our action plans to truly make a mark with [project]." Draw on their desire for a good reputation and high energy.

- **With a Caretaker boss, try:** "You always put the team's best interests first, which is why I'd like to talk about getting stronger advocacy from you at the leadership level" or "I feel like there's tension between us that's gone unaddressed. If we get things out in the open, it'll go a long way to helping me feel more motivated to tackle the challenges ahead." Connect with their inherent drive to support you and others, keep the peace, and restore harmony.

- **With a Controller boss, try:** "To make sure everything is running smoothly and as it should, I'd like to have an honest conversation with you about something that's been on my mind for a while" or "I know you think a lot about how to optimize our processes, and I wanted to chat about how we do that when it comes to trying new ideas." Appeal to their love for logic and systems.

Easing into the feedback conversation isn't about softening the blow; rather, it's about syncing what you have to say with your boss's self-image and worldview, called ego-involvement in psychology. By using this tactic from the start, you can more easily slip past their defenses and communicate in a way they'll pay attention to, which is especially important when your feedback is about touchy topics like their personality or interpersonal style.

Get to the Heart of the Matter

Now that your boss is actually listening, it's time to dive in. Don't unload every single issue you've been storing up like a squirrel with nuts. Circle back to the ABCs you crafted earlier. You want to deliver your feedback in such a way that it acknowledges the specific behavior (B) and directly segues into the desired change (C), completely putting aside your assumption (A). Remember in chapter 3 when we talked about offering a path forward? The same strategy applies here. The best feedback involves setting aside the past, which can't be changed, putting a clear, forward-looking, constructive idea on the table, and then opening the floor for your boss's input, thoughts, or concerns. Here's what this might sound like in common situations:

→ *You're facing unclear expectations:* I noticed that in the kickoff meetings for our last two projects, the scope wasn't sufficiently defined, which left me confused about what I owned. It was unclear who was driving [task] and that led to me redoing work. Creating a project brief that outlines goals and specific deliverables, and reviewing it together at the start, could really help. How do you feel about adding this to our process?

→ *You're not getting approvals or information on time:* We've hit a few snags lately where I find myself waiting on the green light for projects or needing specific details to move forward. Like with the budget approvals, we were in a bit of a holding pattern. How about we introduce a fast track for certain types of approvals so you know what's truly important and needs your immediate attention?

→ *You're getting mixed messages:* In the past month, there have been a few times when the guidance I received from you on how to tackle client feedback differed from that provided by the marketing department. These types of discrepancies make it hard for me to decide on the best next steps. Here's the criteria I've been using to make those judgment calls. What am I missing?

→ *Your boss doesn't follow through:* You mentioned that you'd include me in the strategy meetings so I can offer more direct input on [area]. I haven't been added to those calls yet, and I've been out of the loop on some crucial decisions. Moving forward, I was thinking it'd be easier for us to pull up our calendars while we're speaking and to add me in real time. That way, it's done and not another thing on your to-do list. What do you think?

→ *Your manager changes directions often:* We've paused our work on the Acme initiative three times in the last quarter to handle other urgent stuff. Each time, it felt like we lost sight of what our big-picture goals are, which will catch up with us when the shareholders ask for metrics. What do you think about setting up a regular check-in, maybe every few weeks, to make sure we're still on track with what really matters to us in the long run?

➡ *You're subjected to long, rambling meetings:* Our brainstorming sessions regularly go over by thirty minutes, which ends up making me late for my client touch-bases. What if we structure our agenda with specific time slots for each topic, and maybe nominate a meeting facilitator to keep us on track?

➡ *Your boss is distracted during conversations:* Sometimes our one-on-ones get a bit derailed by notifications popping up. How about we try making those meetings a tech-free time? It could give us more space to think and talk things through without interruptions.

Notice how the scripts above depersonalize the situation— focusing on the task or the issue versus the individual. This metaphorically puts you both on the same side of the table instead of pitting you against each other, changing the dynamic from "me versus you" to "us against the problem." They also stick almost entirely to "I" statements rather than "you" statements and avoid adjectives like "overbearing," "demanding," "weak," and "sensitive," which can come off as character attacks.

Get Their Side of the Story

Even the most enlightened bosses will need a second to process input, so you shouldn't expect an overwhelmingly positive response on the spot. If you've proposed a solution, and your boss has listened and perhaps even affirmed your concerns or asked you for clarification, it's time for some upward empathy, which, simply put, means connecting to what the situation feels like for your boss—and what they need from you. Now is the moment to give them the floor. Ask about challenges contributing to the issues you've raised or that are standing in the way of the solution you've proposed:

- If there are pressures from above that are making this difficult, I'd like to understand. Maybe we can come up with strategies to deal with them.

- I recognize that there might be factors at play here that I'm not aware of. Could you share more about the big picture and what you're dealing with?

- I know you face a lot of complexities, and what I see is only one piece of a larger puzzle. What do you think would be the best way for us to tackle these underlying issues together?

Your boss may reveal that they're facing anything from unexpected budget cuts and suddenly shifting priorities to dealing with conflicts among upper management or even personal issues. So while you may be offering feedback to solve your *own* problem, by presenting yourself as more of a partner than an employee, you could solve a problem for *them* as a result. Offer validation, but more important, propose to help ease their burden:

- Hearing about everything you're juggling really puts things into perspective. Is there a specific area where I could relieve some of the pressure? I'm ready to step up.

- I really appreciate your trusting me and opening up about what you're facing. You're dealing with more than I realized, and I can only imagine how challenging that must be. I'm more than willing to help with X if it would lighten your load.

- I know you've got a lot on your plate, and it makes sense why [issue] has taken a back seat. Why don't I do X on your behalf to get the ball rolling again?

Turning feedback into real change requires agreement on next steps and a shared commitment to follow through. After you offer a solution, your boss might say, "That's something I can do," which makes it easy to cement the next steps. You can also directly ask, "Can I count on you to [specific action]?" or propose a way of gently reminding them to take the feedback into account moving forward, such as "If I notice you're not providing clear direction, how would you prefer I bring that up?" In some cases, it might make sense to propose checking in on progress: "Let's see how things go, and I can make a note to revisit this discussion in eight weeks." It's also wise to follow up with an email, thanking them for being open to the conversation and briefly outlining any agreed-upon actions so there's a clear record.

STEAL THESE SCRIPTS

When your boss says this . . .	Try this . . .
I don't know why you're making such a big deal of this.	I'm not here to exaggerate or create unnecessary drama. But the fact is that [behavior] is affecting my work and, by extension, my ability to deliver on [responsibility].
I'm swamped. I don't have time for this.	I get that we're all stretched thin right now. But I'm still concerned that if we don't address this soon, it might end up taking more of our time down the line. Is there a chance we could make time for a quick discussion, even if it's just to set the stage for a longer chat later?
It doesn't matter to me what you think.	I won't lie, that's hard to hear. I was under the impression that feedback could help us both. Maybe I've got it wrong, though. Is there a way I can share my thoughts that might be more helpful?

When your boss says this . . .	Try this . . .
I'm not the only one who misses deadlines around here.	I agree it's an area we can all improve on, including me. My concern is specifically about how shifts in your deadlines have a ripple effect. If we could find a way to minimize delays on your end, it would help us reach [goal].
I've been doing things this way for years, and nobody's complained before.	I respect the fact that you have a tried and tested way of doing X. I see an opportunity for even better results if we try Y, and I'm wondering if we could build on the foundation you already have.
Well, if we're telling the truth here, then I had a few issues with your approach to X as well.	I'm open to your feedback, and we should get some time on the calendar for that conversation, but for today, let's concentrate on resolving the concerns I've raised. We can schedule a separate time to focus solely on your thoughts about X.
Sure, whatever you say. Clearly you're the boss around here!	I was hoping that sharing my thoughts could help us figure out how we can work better together. Maybe we table this for another time.

Beyond the Conversation

Let the Situation Settle

Once you've said your piece, allow space for your leader to digest your conversation and make the necessary adjustments. For feedback that involves minor change, give it at least two weeks before casting judgment. For more significant shifts, a month or more may be necessary. If your input was related to a specific project, wait until it's over or at least until you hit the next milestone to assess whether your boss has taken your input on board.

The responsibility often falls on you, as the person in a position of lower authority, to track progress and offer soft course corrections. And as the one who gave the feedback, you're going to be more alert to any changes (or the lack thereof). Sure, it can be frustrating to shoulder this extra responsibility, but remind yourself: The changes you're advocating for likely benefit not just you but your team and possibly the entire company.

In most situations, it's enough to track progress by using simple strategies like bookmarking or starring emails and messages that show either positive growth or areas needing improvement. Or you might take quick notes on your phone, dedicating ten minutes each week to jot down observations or have informal chats with colleagues to gauge their perceptions. Here are a few ways to follow up on course corrections:

- I remember we talked about trying [specific action]. I think it could really help with [issue]. Are you still on board with giving that a try?

- We had a great chat about making changes regarding [specific feedback]. I've been keeping an eye out, and it seems like we're still a bit off track with [issue]. What if we try [adjustment]? It might help address it directly.

- It looks like [specific feedback] hasn't fully taken hold, especially around [issue]. Could we talk about what's getting in the way?

Accentuate the Positive

Even when you nail the delivery, giving upward feedback can still cause a relational rupture—awkwardness, tension, or vulnerability because you or your boss feel exposed. Focusing on repair through positive reinforcement is key. When you point out something your manager is doing well or acknowledge the effort they've put into adjusting, it goes a long way toward mending any strain the feedback might have introduced. Just make sure it's genuine and not patronizing:

- When you did [specific action] last time, it made a huge difference.

- I appreciate how open you've been to hearing my thoughts, and I noticed you've started implementing what we discussed. That means a lot.

- I know [new method] hasn't been perfect, but the progress is really encouraging. I admire how well you've [specific action] given everything you're juggling.

Dishing out praise to your boss can do wonders, and not just when you're smoothing things over after offering criticism. Like anyone else, leaders crave recognition. "Sincerely thanking others for their thoughtfulness or effort is extremely effective," one reader told me. "Leaders shoulder a lot of responsibility, but never get compliments. They mostly receive complaints from their bosses and others. Praising the senior managers around me has meant I get a more engaged response when I reach out in the future. They're more willing to help me." This reader's experience speaks to the fact that up to 53 percent of VPs and directors and 42 percent of senior managers want more appreciation from their teams. It makes sense because recognition lights up the same brain pathways as monetary rewards. For the best results, aim to offer five positive pieces of feedback for each critical one. Try these scripts:

- Your ability to put things in perspective has inspired me, and it's a skill I use with my own team now.

- Your input on my report helped me see things from a different angle and made the final product much better.

- Watching you negotiate with senior leadership was a great learning moment for me.

Go Nuclear

If after following the steps in this chapter, you find yourself at an impasse with no sign of progress or willingness to engage from your boss, consider escalation as a last resort. Keep a detailed record of the feedback you've provided (when, where, and exactly what you said), along with any reactions from your boss, and any attempts you've made to follow up or clarify your points. If the situation directly impacts your team's project delivery or dynamics, if you share a good rapport with upper management, or if your company culture supports open communication, reaching out to your boss's boss could be the right move. But if the issue is a violation of company policies, if it deals with sensitive matters like harassment, or if previous attempts to address it within the hierarchy have failed, HR is the better go-to. No matter the issue, try framing your outreach along these lines:

> I'm seeking guidance on a persistent issue that I've been unable to resolve despite my best efforts. Over [time frame], I've provided feedback to my boss about [behavior], aiming for [specific action]. Despite multiple attempts to suggest solutions, including [list them], the situation remains unchanged and now [negative impacts]. I'd like your support on how to proceed.

What to Do When . . .

You Face Retaliation

Unfortunately, after you give feedback or escalate the matter, your boss may try to get back at you—excluding you from meetings, stripping you of certain responsibilities, or increasingly scrutinizing your work. While you should ideally report this to HR (who is typically trained to handle retaliation with discretion and fairness), here's what else you can do to protect yourself:

- **Discreetly document.** Casually confirm decisions or comments by saying, "To make sure I've got this right . . ." and then follow up with an email summarizing these points. Use read receipts or delivery confirmation when sending critical emails, especially those outlining issues or seeking clarification. Volunteer to take minutes in meetings so you can somewhat control the narrative that's shared with others.

- **Collect acknowledgments.** Positive words from clients, colleagues, and other managers are hard to argue against and can be a strong defense against unjust criticism or actions. Use digital collaborative tools (Slack, Microsoft Teams, Asana, Google Docs) so your contributions and the acknowledgments of others are automatically captured. This not only serves as self-promotion (chapter 7) but also can counteract any unfounded claims.

- **Bring it to a bigger audience.** If your boss criticizes or questions your work in a one-on-one setting, say, "I think it'd be useful to get more perspective on this, so I'll bring it up in the next team meeting" or "Before I make the changes you're asking for I'm going to run this by [person/department] as well."

- **Don't sit back in the face of sidelining.** Proactively check in with your co-workers to stay updated. Offer your help or insights with projects. Use social media to highlight what you're working on. If others see what you're doing and know what you have to offer it's tougher for your boss to isolate you.

- **Push back on petty criticisms.** Nudge your boss to give you input at the level you're seeking: "I get that you don't care for the yellow palette, but we haven't reached the point where we're ready to discuss changes to the color scheme. I'm open to your suggestions about the aesthetic from a 10,000-foot level, though." Responses like "My experience has been different. What's an example?" or

"I'm confused. How did you arrive at that conclusion?" force your boss to articulate their rationale.

Someone Says Something Offensive

Your boss calls something "ghetto," a male colleague refers to female associates as "the girls," a senior leader remarks, "Diwali? Ramadan? I can't keep these weird holidays straight." It's one thing to overhear bigoted, discriminatory, or ignorant remarks—and another thing entirely to be on the receiving end. Whether you're the target or an observer, speak up using the following tips:

- **Nip it in the bud.** If it's a colleague or your boss, and you have a strong relationship with them, you can be more direct: "I'm sorry, but I can't let that comment slide. It's biased and not appropriate" or "I'm not okay with you calling me [term]." With an executive or a superior, tread more lightly, say with "Let's avoid generalizations and focus on the facts" or "I have to ask that we keep our discussions free of comments like that. As a person of color, it makes me uncomfortable to hear you say [offensive remark]."

- **Put them on the spot.** Ask a question like "Can you explain what you mean that I'm too emotional in meetings? Because I'm not sure I understand" or "What specifically do you think leads others to see her as aggressive?" You can also appeal to the person's values: "I know you care about giving everyone a fair chance to be successful, but claiming I have too many family responsibilities to get ahead here undermines that." Often, simply saying,

"Could you repeat that?" can prompt someone to rethink the repercussions of their words.

- **Provide an alternative.** Offer them a more respectful way to express the same idea: "Instead of saying, 'That idea is crazy,' you could say, 'That idea is really ambitious' to make the same point." You can also share your own experiences: "I've discovered that the term 'powwow' can be offensive. What if we just say 'discussion'?"

- **Bring it up privately.** Sometimes you may be taken aback in the moment and left speechless. Other times you may need space to cool off, collect your thoughts, or pinpoint why a comment didn't sit right with you. You can later circle back and say something like "I wanted to chat about what you mentioned yesterday about our younger employees and handling pressure. I'm concerned it may unintentionally set the wrong tone with the team. I'd like to find a way to delegate work without age being a factor. Thoughts?"

- **Force a perspective shift.** Turn the tables on them: "If I suggested that your accent made you sound unintelligent, how would that make you feel?" or "Imagine I questioned your skills because of where you went to school. Would that sit well with you?" Sharing a story highlighting the impact of offensive comments to make it relatable and tangible can work better with those in power: "Once I took part in an icebreaker exercise that used ethnic stereotypes as part of the game. It was clear how off-putting it was for almost everyone."

Few projects go off without a hitch, and none of us is always at our best. A quick chat early on about how to handle disagreements can surprisingly make upward (or lateral) feedback much safer, easier, and straightforward. Get out in front of potential issues: "Along the way we'll inevitably have different thoughts on how to manage/approach/tackle things. How do you want to handle that?" Getting good at giving feedback, especially to your boss, takes practice and a genuine desire to work well together. Take a little time each week to spot what's going well, and then tactfully address what's not by using what you've learned in this chapter. After a while, your boss will likely begin to understand your perspective better, trust your judgment more, and value your ability to speak truth to power. You'll become known more broadly as someone who is thoughtful and constructive, and that reputation can open doors and make it easier to build new connections, which is exactly what we'll discuss in the next chapter.

CHAPTER SIX

The Networking Conversation

Build a bench of valuable connections and advocates

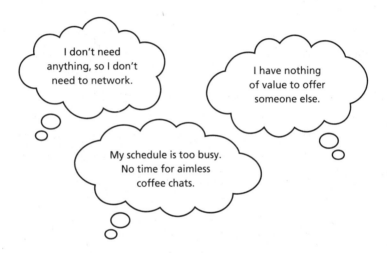

As a UK market analyst for a worldwide technology consulting firm, Leticia spent long hours alone poring over metrics and reports. Much of her work required independent research, which was intellectually stimulating, but the company's size—combined with the fact that Leticia only went into the London offices one or two days a week—made her feel like a cog in the machine.

"I just got an email that several of my international colleagues have been selected for an advanced analytics training program that I would have *loved* being part of," Leticia explained as we started our session. When she asked her boss, whom she trusted greatly, why he hadn't mentioned it or recommended her, he explained, "I didn't know that the program was open to UK analysts."

Though Leticia enjoyed working with him, she realized that she had come to rely on her manager too heavily for information and support for her career. "I've always seen our tight-knit team in the UK as an asset, but during the chitchat before our quarterly meeting, I realized that my counterparts in other countries actually know each other. I've never been great at building relationships, but if I don't start, I know I'll miss another opportunity."

I asked Leticia to brainstorm how she might get to know both her colleagues and new people better. "Well, I'm a natural synthesizer, so I could curate and post a weekly list of 'must-reads' to our internal Women in Tech channel." To Leticia's surprise, the roundup received a positive response almost immediately. One exchange with Imogen, a project manager in a different business unit, sparked a back-and-forth. Though Imogen was based in Los Angeles, she had started out in London, so Leticia sent an email proposing a Zoom chat. "I've often dreamed of moving abroad," she wrote, "but it would be hard to do without a job lined up. Would you mind telling me more about how you managed the transfer and what it looked like behind the scenes?" Imogen agreed, and during their conversation, she repeatedly referred to Sophie, an HR manager Imogen described as "a wizard with visas and relocation." At the end of the call, Leticia thanked Imogen for being so frank and asked if she could connect her to Sophie. Three months later, after working with Sophie and in consultation with her boss, Leticia came to our meeting with a huge smile across her face. "I'm moving to California!" she exclaimed. "I signed an offer from the U.S. team yesterday. I start in three weeks!

"I should have done all of this relationship building two years ago," Leticia told me as we finished up, "but now I finally understand the importance of *the networking conversation*."

The networking conversation is how you build social capital, the currency you earn and spend in the workplace, not in dollars and cents, but in access to information, resources, and more. Having allies who can give you the lowdown about how things actually happen, let you know who is really in charge, and tip you off to intel you'd otherwise be unaware of allows you to be more effective and proactive about all the conversations in this book so far. Plus, managing up isn't just about influencing your boss—it's about strategically building and leveraging relationships across your organization. With a strong network, not only can you bypass bureaucracy and expand your ability to secure money, people, space, and other assets that'll make your job easier, you'll also gain a more well-rounded understanding of internal dynamics—unspoken rules, upcoming changes, and power shifts.

But like Leticia, maybe you've pushed the networking conversation to the bottom of your priority list, only to discover that you have no one to turn to when you need a quick piece of advice on navigating company politics, an introduction to a potential client, or insights into a new market. In the long run, this can put you in a precarious position where you might find yourself sideswiped by major organizational changes, at the mercy of red tape, or worse.

In this chapter, we'll deal with the natural awkwardness of putting yourself out there without feeling like you've gone back to middle school. First, you've got to expose yourself to new people. But no one wants to feel like they're ingratiating themselves or appearing overeager when it comes to building relationships, so you'll get specific scripts and strategies to reach out without coming off as a suck-up. Perhaps most important, I'll walk you through exactly how to have a networking discussion in a way that feels more like a meeting of the minds and less like you're begging for favors. We'll cover different mechanics and considerations of how to make a request without asking for too much and turning the person off—and ensuring each connection leads to long-term growth, not just immediate gain.

The networking conversation marks an important turning point: You're not simply improving or coping with the situation you're in, but you're actively creating your future. It sets the stage for the visibility conversation (chapter 7) because when influential figures recognize your name, it elevates your status and makes them take your accomplishments more seriously. They may invite you to important meetings where you can contribute and be noticed by senior leaders or promote your ideas in front of others. This recognition can then open doors to opportunities with the advancement conversation (chapter 8), including recommending you for a new role or promotion that's not yet advertised. Forget about climbing the corporate ladder one handshake at a time and think instead about building a web of connections where help can come from any direction.

Expose Yourself

It may sound obvious, but you can't have the networking conversation unless you have people to talk to. Thanks to the mere-exposure effect, the more someone encounters you (even in small ways), the more likely they are to develop a connection with you. Here are a few ways to put yourself in the path of those you want to build a connection with:

- Join an affinity group to meet people from different departments or levels of seniority who share similar interests or backgrounds.

- Volunteer for cross-functional projects or task forces to understand the broader business and create relationships with other colleagues.

- Participate in an internal book club that provides a forum to share ideas and learn from one another.

- Post on company-wide forums to chat with others across the organization.

- Take the elevator instead of the stairs, or grab coffee from a different spot, if it means you're more likely to bump into someone new or influential.

- Sit near decision-makers during meetings or facing the door so that it's easier to strike up conversations.

- Attend company outings, team-building events, or after-work meet-ups.

Wherever you are in your career, remember that you won't have the time or energy to build alliances with everyone, so when it comes to networking, consider engaging with:

- **Decision-makers.** Spoiler alert: Your boss is one of many people who can decide your career trajectory. Your manager's peers, leaders in different departments, and even clients, board members, or external partners can be great people to have in your corner.

- **Powerful peers.** Colleagues from a different location you occasionally bump into, members of cross-functional project teams you work with a few times a year—any one of them has the potential to lend a hand when you need it.

- **Behind-the-scenes badasses.** This includes support and administrative staff, such as IT, accounting, HR, and facilities. While often overlooked, they can be invaluable sources for insider knowledge and can pull strings when you need a favor.

Finally, when strategizing your networking approach, consider power differentials and the level of access you have to higher-ups. In smaller companies (5 to 100 employees) it's feasible that you could be known by and in touch with top executives, but if you're early in your career at a large organization (150 to several thousand employees), don't bank on grabbing coffee with the CEO anytime soon. Take cues from the company culture as well. Do senior staff favor an open-door policy or stick to formal communication? Look for signs of their willingness to connect, like striking up small talk or showing interest in your work. Organizational shake-ups like mergers or management shifts often reveal chances for networking as roles and attitudes evolve.

STEAL THESE SCRIPTS

You never get a second chance to make a first impression, so you'll need to be ready with a compelling introduction at all times to demonstrate that you're competent and likable. Fill in the blanks below to set yourself apart. In the next chapter, you'll learn how to craft a longer, more story-driven version of your bio that highlights your accomplishments.

Short introduction for company gatherings, events, and casual or chance encounters

Template: Nice to meet you! I'm [your name]. I work in [department/team] with [boss], focusing on [key projects / initiatives]. How about you?

In practice: Nice to meet you! I'm Jimmy. I work in corporate responsibility with Abigail, making sure everything we do here at Acme Corp is better for the environment. What brings you to this conference?

Longer introduction for meetings, all-hands, and other more structured situations

Template: I'm [your name], [your job title]. I have a background in [area of expertise] and now I help [your target audience] understand/do/achieve [result], so that [why it matters]. Currently I'm working on / responsible for [key initiatives], which have / will [outcome].

In practice: Hi, I'm Jimmy, a corporate responsibility analyst here at Acme Corp. I have a background in environmental studies, and now I help our operations team make our manufacturing processes more sustainable so that we can reduce costs while doing our part to prevent climate change. Currently I'm working on a risk assessment of our factories, which will inform our annual road map.

Master the Art of Asking

What do you say to convince a new contact to meet with you for a connection call, coffee, or lunch without sounding desperate or presumptuous? How do you ask for help without coming off as self-serving or making the other person feel exploited? You may never be best friends with everyone in your network, but these connections don't have to be purely transactional. When done right, you can form genuine, reciprocal relationships that are a source of support *and* meaningful career clout now and into the future.

Drill Down to a Small Ask

Busy people have to be selective about where to focus their energy, so if you approach someone in power with zero idea of what you're looking for or where you're trying to go, it can be a major turnoff. A better strategy is to decide ahead of time what you want so that they can quickly assess the situation and decide if they can—or want to—help.

Instead of inventing a contrived reason to meet, consider a minor request to justify meeting in real time. Smaller asks typically require minimal time, effort, or reputational risk and are specific in nature, usually involving access to information in one way or another. Use the examples below as inspiration to pick one manageable info-ask you can make when you meet:

- Seeking insights into trends your contact is seeing that have not yet hit the mainstream

- Learning best practices and proven strategies for being successful in your role

- Mining for unspoken details about the company culture

- Discovering how work is proposed, reviewed, and approved within the organization

- Uncovering historical context about projects or relationships that allows you to circumvent tricky politics

- Requesting their take on an upcoming change that could impact your team

- Asking about progress on a recent initiative and what's working or not

- Getting them to share templates or sample decks their team developed

- Securing an introduction or a referral to another department, a higher-level leader, or a client

- Sourcing vendor or supplier recommendations

- Finding out how to borrow special software, equipment, or meeting space

- Researching the best way to access exclusive analytics, market research, or other databases

- Gaining intel on leveraging corporate partnerships or unused budget and underutilized personnel

- Joining early testing groups for products or services in development by the company so you and your team are on the bleeding edge of innovation

While your long-term goal might be some type of career sponsorship, don't make the mistake of asking someone you barely know for something significant like a new job or a large sum of money right out of the gate. That's like proposing marriage on a first date—it's an abrupt leap that can appear aggressive or clueless because it bypasses the gradual nature of relationship building.

Get on Their Calendar

If you're not going to bump into your contact soon, you'll likely need to email them to ask for a meeting, but this isn't as simple as it seems. The average worker receives more than 120 new emails each day, but responds to only 25 percent of them. And for an executive, that steady stream of messages might be a deluge. Yours needs to grab their attention right away, starting with your subject line. Aim for no more than thirty to sixty characters so it's scannable across most devices. Try these approaches:

- **Personalizing to catch their eye.** "[Their first name], connecting about [topic]" or "[Their first name], question about [topic]"

- **Name-dropping a mutual connection.** "Following up from [event]" or "[Contact] said to ping you"

- **Mentioning something you have in common.** "Fellow women's group member" or "Exploring common ground in [area]"

- **Referencing something they've done.** "Inspired by your leadership on [project]" or "Loved your presentation on [topic]"

Busy people are skimmers. Send a wall of text and they'll glaze over your message, never coming back to it. Limit the body of your message to around two hundred words. Likewise, steer clear of ambiguous phrases like "I'd love to meet and chat," which lack direction, and phrases like "I'd love to pick your brain," which can sound opportunistic. Be specific about why you want to connect, any mutual connections you have, or specific work of theirs that you admire. If there's a practical way you can help them in return, highlight it. Maybe sharing your perspective on a topic, providing feedback on a project, or offering to make an introduction. But don't force a value proposition if there isn't a clear fit. That can come off as insincere or like you're overcompensating.

Here's what the pitch you put together might sound like (see "Steal These Scripts" for more!):

Subject: Thanks [their first name]—[project] strategies
Hi [their first name],
   Thanks again for speaking to [team] earlier this week. I was in the room seated next to [mutual contact] and appreciated what you had to say about [topic]. I'm currently leading a similar initiative focused on [area]. Over the last three months, we've run into an

issue with [specific challenge]. Given your expertise in this
area, would you be open to a twenty-minute call next week?
Understanding how you've navigated these roadblocks would
be invaluable. I'd also be happy to share my knowledge in
[specialty], if you believe that would be useful for your work
on [project].

Should you suggest specific times to meet or send a calendar
booking link when trying to schedule? Preferences on this can vary
widely, so follow what's common in your company culture. If
you're unsure, propose three to five options and indicate your flexibility, especially if you're the person with lower positional authority: "I'm available the following times next week, but I'm also
happy to accommodate your schedule. I could also meet virtually
if that's easier."

If your contact declines a call or meet-up, pat yourself on the
back for trying and move on. Circumstances change, and the opportunity to connect might present itself again in the future. You
can also use the strategies later in this chapter to further build rapport and make it possible they'd be open to your request in the future. If you haven't received a response within ten days to two
weeks, a gentle follow-up is okay, but limit yourself to no more
than two follow-ups total.

STEAL THESE SCRIPTS

You might be thinking, "Couldn't I just ask for what I need over email without having to meet them live?" You could, but don't. When you're on a call or in person, you can express highly contagious *positive* emotions like enthusiasm and interest more genuinely and vividly than you can asynchronously, accelerating a connection and prompting the other person to invest in helping you.

Get an executive's insight on the company culture

Subject: Great article on [topic]
Hi [their first name],

I came across your article on [topic] in this month's company newsletter and was impressed by your perspective on [trend], especially [unique angle]. As someone who has been at [company] for years, it's clear you have deep knowledge on how things work here. I'm relatively new to [team] and would love to hear more about how you've navigated [company] culture to reach your level of success. Are you available for lunch in the coming weeks? I'm happy to offer some times and locations, or I can work around your schedule.

Have a cross-functional colleague get you an "in" with a powerful client

Subject: Found you via [source]
Hi [their first name],

Good to be in touch. I came across your name a few times while thumbing through past documents for [client/account] and thought I'd reach out. I'm going to be doing more work with them beginning next quarter and I'd love to learn from your experiences and seek your guidance about connecting with [key contact at client]. Could we grab a coffee next Thursday?

Feel out if your boss's peer has a team member you can snag for your own project

Subject: Collaborating on [key objective]
Hi [their first name],

[Your boss's name] suggested I reach out to you directly, since our team has been putting together a road map for the next six months. I know we've been in a number of meetings together, but since we haven't had the opportunity to connect one-on-one yet, would you be open to a call? I can share our plan and I'd love to get your thoughts on how we can work together to optimize the resources available to both of our teams.

Open Strong

When it comes to networking meetings, most people want to have a sense of what to expect. Sending a formal agenda for a fifteen-to-thirty-minute connection call or a lunch (which, based on most social norms, is meant to be more casual) might be overkill, but a confirmation note expressing your enthusiasm and setting a light intention for the conversation is perfectly appropriate: "Looking forward to coffee on Thursday! I'm hoping we can touch on [topic]." Not only does a quick message demonstrate right off the bat that you're not going to waste their time, it helps them be more open, relaxed, and focused on the topic at hand.

Remember, *you* initiated this meeting, so it's *your* responsibility to guide the dialogue. Passive comments like "I don't really have a specific agenda, I just thought it'd be nice to chat" or "I'm not sure what to talk about, but I'm just happy to be here" make you look unprepared. On the other hand, excessive awe and gratitude (e.g., "I can't believe you'd take time out of your busy schedule for me!") might seem polite, but actually place you in a subservient position. Stick to "meeting of the minds" language like "I'm so glad we can chat today," "I appreciate us being able to connect like this," or "It's wonderful to have this time together."

For shorter meetings (thirty minutes or less), limit small talk to two or three minutes to maximize the time for the rest of your discussion. Five to ten minutes is appropriate for meetings of one hour or more. A formal office setting or virtual format usually calls for a quicker transition to the topic at hand, while a relaxed coffee shop meet-up lends itself to a bit more chitchat. Pay attention to your contact's demeanor, though. If they're known to be more reserved or strictly business-oriented—or if you notice them giving short answers and seeming distracted or antsy—then shift gears.

Make the Most of Your Main Interaction

Once it's time to get down to business, look for a natural lull in small talk to respectfully transition into your topic by:

- **Acknowledging your schedules.** "I want to be conscious of our time together today. Would it be all right if we turn our discussion toward [topic]?" or "I'm mindful that we both have other commitments, so if you don't mind, let's pivot to [topic]."

- **Calling out the awkwardness.** "I realize we're jumping topics, but as I mentioned in my email, getting your thoughts on X would be helpful" or "At the risk of taking a sharp turn in our conversation, I'd love to transition and talk about [topic]."

- **Drawing an association.** "You just mentioned X, which actually ties into what I wanted to discuss today, which is [topic]" or "I wanted to say congrats again on [achievement]. It's been inspiring and it's somewhat related to what I'm hoping to chat about, which is [topic]."

It's then a good idea to provide a bit of context about your situation (no more than one to three minutes) and why you're specifically seeking *their* help or guidance, before posing a question about your info-ask. Use one of the following scripts:

- I'm transitioning to [new team] soon. It's an exciting opportunity, but I'm nervous about getting up to speed quickly. I know you've worked with [your boss / collaborators] before. Are there specific areas you'd suggest I focus on in the first ninety days?

- I'm looking for seasoned graphic designers who specialize in [area] for [project]. I was chatting with [mutual connection], who said you have a real knack for finding great people. Based on your experience, where's the best place to start when looking to hire high-quality contractors?

- I'm gearing up to take on [responsibility], which will
  involve a lot of financial modeling. In our company-wide
  meetings, I've been impressed with the analyses your
  team presents. So I'd love to know: How did you go
  about gathering the data to inform those reports?

As is the case for other conversations in this book, you'll be more
successful by listening more than you talk. The more someone else
shares about their experiences, knowledge, and skills, the more they'll
like you because it triggers the pleasure centers of their brain.
Sprinkle in short anecdotes from your experience along the way
that build credibility and make the conversation feel like a back-
and-forth versus an interrogation: "That rings true to my experience as well. What I found leading [area/responsibility] is [insight].
How does that match up with what you've seen?" or "I'm plugged
into the [specialty] community and I've been hearing that X is an
up-and-coming trend, too."

Keep your ears open for natural moments to introduce an additional or bigger ask or clues as to where the relationship might go
in the future, bearing in mind that it's still early and you want to
focus on seeking information rather than asking for a favor. For
example, say you want to find funding for something you're working on and the colleague you're speaking with mentions they're
going to end the year with unused budget. Ask about it: "Hearing
about your surplus got me thinking. What usually happens with
that money?" Or if your goal is to get the scoop on an upcoming
company restructure and a leader from another team alludes to
personnel changes they're making, you could follow up with "I appreciate your candor and sharing that our sales have been lower.
What are your thoughts on how that's going to trickle down to our
staff and projects?"

Framing your questions around your contact's experiences or decisions (e.g., "Do you think it's possible . . . ?" or "How would you suggest going about . . . ?") subtly acknowledges their expertise and judgment, building your social capital. You may also find that they volunteer to help you!

Close with Confidence

If you're booked for a set time block, stick to it and keep your eye on the clock. Letting the meeting go over could imply you either mismanage time or take theirs for granted. Here's a smooth way to wrap up: "I see we're coming up to the top of the hour. This has been so valuable. What you shared about [one to three key points] was really useful." Then end with a call to action rather than letting the conversation meekly fizzle out with "Uh, well . . . thanks again. Bye!" Set the stage for an ongoing relationship, basing your choice on the following factors:

- **If your contact seemed disinterested, gave short responses, checked the time a lot, or mentioned they're in a rush.** Express interest in staying in touch without demanding an immediate commitment: "I'll add you on LinkedIn and maybe we can revisit [topic] at some point in the future."

- **If you already asked for assistance in the conversation.** Don't push it with yet another request. Thank them and own the follow-up: "I appreciate your willingness to introduce me to [leader]. I'll circle back with a sample email you can send on my behalf."

- **If your original ask is no longer relevant to what was discussed, but the conversation otherwise flowed well.** Adjust your request based on the new information that's come to light: "Your point about [new information] was eye-opening. Before we go, I was initially interested in [original ask], but now I see [adapted ask] might make more sense. Would you be open to guiding me on this?"

If all goes according to plan—meaning the other person showed genuine enthusiasm throughout the conversation, offered their help proactively, and your chat touched on topics or challenges related to your original ask—then you have a pretty solid foundation upon which to make a direct request for a follow-up meeting, concrete assistance, or both, while acknowledging their discretion and autonomy to say no. Here are a few ways to make your pitch:

- As we touched on today, I've been developing a proposal to launch a company-wide mental health day. I've reached a stage where an endorsement from a leader like you could help it get buy-in from the CEO. Can I send you a one-pager that outlines the goals and potential impact? Regardless of whether you're a yes or no, I've valued everything you've shared with me today.

- You mentioned having a lot of experience with [area]. Would you be willing to share any reports or datasets that could inform what I'm working on? Of course I'd attribute you in any slides, but I also understand if that information is proprietary.

- It's been great learning about your background in hyperlocal marketing. I'm actually exploring partnerships with local businesses, similar to what you've done in the past. How would you feel about setting up a separate time to chat about how we might get you involved with our onboarding process for landing those first three contracts? Even if now isn't the right time, the invitation will be open to collaborate on this later, too.

If they respond positively, amazing! Express your gratitude and follow up within one business day with the specifics they've agreed to. For instance, if they agreed to review your proposal, send it promptly along with a brief, appreciative note reiterating how much their support means to you. Got a lukewarm or noncommittal response? Give them space: "I know you may need to look at your calendar and see if this is something you can commit to. What if I follow up in two weeks to check in?" If you get rejected, that's okay. Thank your contact for considering the request and reinforce how valuable your conversation was: "I totally understand! It was helpful just to discuss these ideas with you." Offering to keep them updated, regardless of their direct involvement, can keep the door open for future interactions without pressuring them to pitch in.

Beyond the Conversation

Build Rapport by Being of Service

The best way to reinvest in any networking relationship is to provide value, even in the smallest of ways. What may seem like an unimportant gesture or inconsequential piece of information to you could be very meaningful to your contacts regardless of whether they are more or less experienced, powerful, or established than you.

Consider one or more of these "micro-gives":

- **Share a resource.** Through a vegan group at her company, Giada discovered that one of her boss's peers (with whom she had had little to no interaction thus far) had recently started composting their vegetable scraps. When Giada came across an interesting composting tool she was considering trying herself, she took a chance and forwarded it to her boss's peer, who replied, "Cool— thanks!" It didn't seem significant at first, but in every meeting afterward, the leader made a point to personally greet Giada and ask about how she was doing, which gave her a chance to have the visibility conversation (chapter 7).

- **Offer an invite.** Organize an internal roundtable or panel discussion featuring a topic your executives care about. Once a quarter, request recommendations for insightful industry news or trends that you send out or post to social media as a roundup, tagging those who contributed. Set up a happy hour for peers across the company.

- **Become a bridge builder.** Look for mutually beneficial connections and introductions you can make. Always do a double opt-in introduction. Reach out to each person separately, with some context as to why you think they would benefit from knowing each other, such as shared interests, potential business opportunities, or relevant skills and experiences. If both parties agree, put them in touch via email, text, etc.

- **Surprise and delight.** When we're surprised, positive emotions like gratitude and connection intensify up to 400 percent. Perhaps you put extra polish on a joint presentation by adding graphics, charts, and other forms of data visualization without being asked. If someone asks you for feedback on something, send a video recording of your input rather than just leaving comments in a doc. If you come across a book your colleague or a leader might enjoy, mail a copy to their office, along with a handwritten note.

When you offer assistance, you activate the "helper's high," sparking "feel good" neurotransmitters like dopamine. Even when people don't remember the specifics of what you did or said, they always remember how you made them feel. Being of service also triggers reciprocity, an innate human desire to want to return favors and balance scales. This isn't transactional or manipulative (especially if you act with kindness and genuine interest in someone else); it's just how social relationships naturally work and evolve.

Keep the Relationship Warm

With few exceptions, you wouldn't ignore a friend for months or years and then expect a favor, right? The same goes for professional contacts. But when work and life get busy and you fall out of touch, it can feel awkward to reach out again. Since networking is a continuous process rather than a one-time event, it helps to create a system to check in with your network and keep your connections alive.

If using a spreadsheet to track your follow-ups feels too cumbersome or over-the-top, there are simpler methods. For example, you can create a special list on your social media platforms for people you want to keep in regular touch with, making it easy to see and engage with their updates, or maybe you set a monthly or quarterly task in your calendar to reach out. After a call with a potential referral source, I set an email reminder to catch up with them again three or so months later using a tool called FollowUpThen. When that reminder hits my inbox, I can either snooze it or take action on it right away, based on my bandwidth at the time. That way my networking efforts are top of mind without overwhelming me.

But what do you say when you reach out again? You might let the person know how their guidance has paid off for you: "I took your advice on [topic], and it really made a difference in [specific outcome]. Thanks for steering me right!" You can also update your contact on what you've been up to, since they may now have more of a vested interest in you. If six months or more have passed since you last spoke, a face-to-face meeting is ideal, if possible, to rekindle the emotional connection that email or text can't match.

Remember, the little things also go a long way, too. For example, say you learn your contact is getting a new pet or they're running a marathon. Check in with them to see how it's going to show you actually care about them as a person, and not only about what they can do for you. A friend of mine did just that, and it paid off. When her colleague's baby was born, my friend was one of the first to congratulate her, thanks to the note she'd put in her calendar. That small gesture helped cement their relationship, and down the line, it even led to the colleague sending my friend some business.

What to Do When . . .

You Want People to Come to You

You often have to be the one making moves to build relationships by attending events, setting up meetings, and reaching out first.

But this can be tiring and downright difficult, especially if you're in a small company where internal networking options are limited. Here's how to attract connections to you, which goes hand in hand with increasing your visibility, which we'll discuss in the next chapter:

- **Level up your LinkedIn profile.** A great photo (full-color, simple background, approachable smile, shot from the chest up) can get you twenty-one times more views and nine times more connections. Customize your headline to showcase your specialty or value proposition. For instance, instead of "Accounting Associate at ABC Company" try "Foreign Tax Prep Pro | Achieving Compliance for International Companies." In both your headline and About section, use relevant keywords to improve your searchability across both LinkedIn and Google.

- **Like and comment.** Whether you invest in LinkedIn or another social platform where your industry hangs out, you don't have to create original content from the outset. It's totally fine—beneficial even—to begin by engaging with others' content first. When you go beyond saying something perfunctory like "Nice article!" and instead offer a reflection or an addition (e.g., "What you said struck me because [reason]. It reminds me of something I once heard . . ."), you'll pique others' curiosity and get more private invitations to connect. Plus, when your comment generates discussion or attracts engagement, the algorithms put it in front of a wider audience, exposing you to even more potential contacts.

- **Publish your own perspectives.** Posting once per week is a great place to start when it comes to creating your own content. You can share commentary on an article you enjoyed, a reflection on a key lesson you've learned in your career, your take on industry trends or news, a case study that showcases a project you've been involved in, an event summary with key takeaways, or a step-by-step how-to guide for a skill related to your expertise. Publish consistently and you'll be seen as an expert and attract the attention of peers and influencers.

- **Find offline watering holes.** Consider joining associations, trade groups, special interest organizations, or your alma mater's alumni group to put yourself in the path of new people, not just within your company but within your industry. By simply showing up to their events and seminars, you create chances for spontaneous interactions that could become valuable connections.

- **Rely on referrals.** Asking existing contacts, "Who else do you think I should know?" or "Who else should I be talking to?" can turn one relationship into several. This strategy helps you grow your network of "weak ties," which research has shown to be more valuable than strong ties in certain contexts, including job searches. Because weak ties serve as a bridge to different social worlds, they can provide access to information and resources that your closest connections can't.

You're Roped In to Office Gossip

The broader and deeper your network, the more you naturally become privy to a wider range of conversations, including the gossipy kind. While this can sometimes be a sign that you're a trusted confidant, trading gossip isn't the same as exchanging information. If you're not careful, it can also be distracting and draining; ultimately, it can undermine people's trust in you. Here's how to rise above the fray:

- **Empathize and redirect.** Validate the gossiper so that they feel seen and heard, then nudge them toward a different subject or a solution. For example, "That's tough. You should talk directly with your boss about this" or "It sounds like the situation is still bothering you, but it's out of your hands. How's the new project you're working on?"

- **Enforce a boundary.** Express your discomfort with phrases like "I don't feel comfortable talking about so-and-so," "I really don't like talking about people's personal matters," "I prefer not to get involved in the rumor mill," or "This subject isn't the best use of our time."

- **Say something complimentary.** Say something positive about the person being attacked. Subtly challenge assumptions or inherent biases: "She doesn't come off as aggressive to me. I admire how she comes to the table with a strong point of view."

- **Signal your disinterest.** Deprive the gossiper of their reward: attention. Complement your words with strong nonverbal signals. Stand up and move toward closing your office door or walk away, or if you're interacting virtually, divert your gaze or start typing. If someone passes a "juicy story" on to you, don't pass it any further. Be the one who acts with integrity.

- **Watch your digital footprint.** After a meeting where Ricardo, a business development manager, presented his team's quarterly earnings report, he was shocked to find that two VPs had been back-channeling and bad-mouthing his boss. Unbeknownst to them, the chat transcript had captured everything—the general group discussion *and* their private messages. The moral of this story? Never put anything in writing that you wouldn't feel comfortable with someone else seeing. Avoid sending emails, texts, or instant messages bad-mouthing anyone, as these can be saved, forwarded, or accessed by others.

Whether you're asking for information or giving it, a strong network is built one relationship at a time. Reflect on one or two ways you could put yourself in the path of new people, or better yet, look around at your current connections with fresh eyes. Maybe there's a leader in a different department you've only spoken to during company-wide meetings or a peer you've casually exchanged emails with but never really engaged in a deeper conversation. Use the scripts from this chapter to reach out and take things further. Often, the best professional relationships come about through a mix of strategy and serendipity, so be open to possibility everywhere. You never know where striking up a conversation while in line at the office cafeteria or sitting next to someone new at an internal training might lead. Once you're known to a broader group of people, you're ready to have the visibility conversation and elevate your access to opportunities, influence, and more.

CHAPTER SEVEN

The Visibility Conversation

Showcase your accomplishments—sans slimy self-promotion

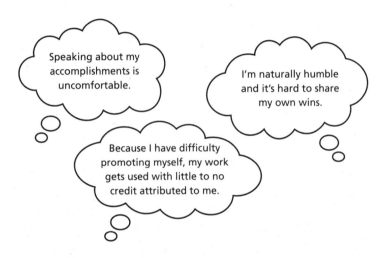

As a pattern maker at a couture fashion house in New York, Jeremy reveled in the precision and detail of his craft. He loved the travel, the constant learning, and the innovation within a centuries-old profession. One week, he'd be hunched over his worktable, carefully stitching together a delicate pattern for the company's new collection. The next, he'd be jetting off to source new fabrics from countries across Asia, filled with gratitude that he could call this "work." After three years at the company, his goal was to become an atelier manager so that he could expand his role beyond pattern making to oversee the entire design process, from initial sketches to the final fittings. Jeremy felt he had a special talent for navigating creative conflict, but he rarely received acknowledgment for the hours he spent creating consensus and quietly guiding the team toward successful, sold-out collections season after season.

One night as Jeremy was heading home for the day, he found himself on the train with Taraji, one of the company's executives. Jeremy had met Taraji at a company holiday party several months earlier, where they struck up a friendly conversation about their shared passion for dogs. A talented designer in her own right, she and Jeremy had spoken two separate times so he could consult with her on the collections, but they never touched on the people-wrangling aspects of Jeremy's job that were going to make him a great atelier manager someday.

"What have you been up to lately?" she asked him with genuine curiosity.

While Jeremy was tempted to tell her about the collections, it had been a long day of playing the middleman between a demanding designer, who had a penchant for pushing the boundaries of what was possible, the meticulous tailors in his department, who put tradition and quality first, and the production team, who were driven by deadlines and cost controls above all else. Just a few minutes before he left the office, they had finally come up with a solution that satisfied everyone. "I had a real breakthrough today with a few of our team members," he said. "They've been arguing for weeks about design versus money, and I finally figured out a way to show them they can have both."

Taraji listened intently, and as her stop approached, she stood up and said, "It's one thing to be great at your craft, but another to be good with people. I'd like to hear more the next time we meet. Email me—let's get something on the calendar."

When Jeremy got home, he announced to his roommate Carmen, "You'll never guess who I just chatted with!"

As Jeremy recounted the conversation with Taraji, Carmen's eyes widened in admiration. "Wow, Jer, you made the most of those five minutes with her! I would just have complained to Taraji, but you highlighted something she would have never known about you otherwise. You really had your story straight."

As he reflected, Jeremy realized that making Taraji aware of the breadth of his abilities and his accomplishments would be an important step toward her becoming a powerful ally who could open doors and advocate for him. While many people know that advocating for themselves is important, few understand that *the visibility conversation* isn't about shameless self-promotion; rather, it's about how you present what you're doing, how you frame the way you're growing from challenges, and how you put your contributions in context of the organization's goals and objectives.

You might be thinking, "I don't want attention; I'd rather be brilliant behind the scenes." Fair, but let me put it this way: Always picking up the slack for colleagues or being your boss's secret weapon without any acknowledgment is a recipe for resentment and burnout. Plus, the type of self-promotion you'll master through this chapter won't turn you into an egocentric spotlight seeker. Instead, through language and frameworks, you'll learn how to talk about yourself in a way that showcases your value to others. Whether it's making a memorable impact in casual workplace encounters, wowing your boss in one-on-ones, or voicing your views in meetings, I'll show you how to identify and articulate achievements hidden in everyday tasks and how to use subtle storytelling skills to relay your results. We'll also touch on more complicated visibility situations, including what to do when someone steals credit for your work, or your boss stands in the way of you receiving the recognition you deserve.

The visibility conversation goes beyond simply listing what you've done. It's about creating a compelling narrative that shapes people's perception of you and solidifies your reputation. This taps into the availability heuristic, which refers to the fact that others judge you based on what they easily remember about you. Imagine you've spent hours improving a process that saves your department thousands each month. If you don't let anyone know, your boss might assume the savings are from the vendor reducing prices, not your hard work. Or consider the times you've stayed late to meet deadlines and keep the team on track. If you don't speak up about your dedication, you might end up doing all the extra work without getting any recognition. On the other hand, each time you share your successes, you reinforce an image of competence and commitment in the minds of your colleagues and superiors. That's the crucial difference between simply being known to people at work—and having a compelling personal brand that positions you for advancement (chapter 8).

Revisit Your One-Year Vision

Before you begin having the visibility conversation, ask yourself, "When I tell others about my work, am I simply listing all of the things I've done in my role? Or am I intentionally highlighting what I want *to do more of* and *want to be known for*?" You want to bring visibility to your promotable work—meaning work that

(1) is central to the strategic direction of your team or company, (2) puts you in the path of key stakeholders, including upper management or external clients, and (3) has potential to impact the company's bottom line. If you continually bring attention to time-consuming tasks that don't excite you or emphasize responsibilities that don't mesh with your career goals, then you could find yourself pigeonholed into a career you don't want or work you dislike.

Consider Charles, a retail store manager, who frequently shared anecdotes about turning around his location's sales numbers. This led to him being assigned to solely underperforming stores and being overlooked to lead the opening of a flagship location, which aligned better with his aspirations to go into merchandising. Or take Maha, a talented young attorney, who often drew attention to her successes in complex court cases. While winning these tough cases built her brand as a strong litigator, the long hours, extensive preparation, and frequent travel they demanded ran counter to her desire for greater work-life balance.

Remember your one-year vision from chapter 1? Not only does it give you a road map for the kind of assignments you want to take on, but it can also provide important clues about the aspects of your work that you want to highlight when you document stories to share and speak about yourself in one-on-ones, cross-functional meetings, and elsewhere (all of which you'll learn how to do next). To use your one-year vision as a filter for the type of work you do—and do not—want to get involved in and talk about, ask yourself:

- **How can I reframe my current or recent contributions to emphasize their relevance to my career goals?** Say you want to manage managers, but you only have one direct report. Use the upcoming strategies to highlight adjacent experiences—how you've resolved conflicts across departments, made decisions under pressure, and built consensus among different stakeholders—to subtly demonstrate to peers and superiors that you have the chops for a higher-level role well before you actually get the job.

- **What opportunities can I create or seek out that will both advance my vision and increase my visibility?** If you want to transition from a software developer to a product manager role, perhaps you seek out a stretch project that allows you to do user research so you can eventually share anecdotes about that rather than complicated coding tasks you've done.

- **Am I already known for the work that will drive me toward my vision?** For example, you want to get away from being a "jack-of-all-trades" marketing associate. You stop telling colleagues they can come to you for "branding, pricing, packaging—whatever's needed!" and start telling them that you're their go-to expert specifically for strategies and insights on community engagement.

While it may seem calculating to think ahead in this way, it's not. We've all been in meetings when someone rambles on about their work in an unfocused, disjointed way that makes you wonder if they know what they're doing. Ditto on conversations when someone goes overboard bragging about a particular project or success in a way that makes you want to roll your eyes. Planning ahead helps you strike the right note in conversations without boring your audience or sounding fake.

Get Your Story Straight

Storytelling is a powerful way to get your achievements across, but you don't have to impress and entertain others by spinning elaborate, grandiose tales. In fact, shorter, more concise stories are often the most effective in the professional context. This could be as straightforward as sharing a brief anecdote about a challenge you overcame or talking about a project you're proud of in a conversation, in a meeting, or even in an email. Listeners are twenty-two times more likely to remember statistics combined with stories than facts alone. What's even more surprising is that when you tell a story, your listener's brain will actually start to sync with yours, a process known as neural coupling. This means that when you substitute "I talked to the vendor about our contract" with "I know revenue has been down this year, so I negotiated a 25 percent discount for the next year to bring us in under budget and offer some positive news we can share with the board," your boss doesn't just *hear* about what you did, but they experience the same positive emotions—excitement, inspiration, and relief—that you felt.

Keep a Story Bank

You might be thinking, "I haven't done anything impressive or noteworthy lately. I definitely don't have anything to tell an interesting story about!" To that, I call bullshit. You just haven't trained yourself to look for and record instances of the smart ways you overcame a challenge, advanced your leadership's priorities, or otherwise scored points for your team or organization. The solution? Keep a story bank. This doesn't have to be fancy. Get started by setting aside fifteen minutes a week to reflect on your big and small wins in a simple, easy-to-access document.

Don't log anything and everything. Be selective. Aim to have four to six stories that you update every other month or quarterly and that clearly sync up with your one-year vision, as well as those of your boss and the organization as a whole. Go beyond the basic details. Connect *what* happened to *why* it matters and *how* you played a role. If you've taken the initiative to tackle a worthwhile problem from the ownership conversation (chapter 3), then you may already have results to speak to when it comes to eliminating bottlenecks, addressing neglected needs, tackling feedback patterns, and more. To expand your thinking further, also consider:

- How have you increased sales, productivity, or volume? How has this helped achieve the company's key performance indicators or targets?

- What processes have you optimized or improved? What metrics point to this increased efficiency or saving money (and how much)?

- Have you assumed new responsibilities that weren't part of your job? Did you complete any special projects and what was the result?

- How have you adapted your work in response to new technologies or trends? What benefits has this created?

- What steps have you taken to generate new business and forge affiliations, partnerships, or strategic alliances— and how have these impacted your team's success?

- When have you met a difficult deadline or brought a project in under budget? What difference did this make?

- What specific expertise or competencies have you
  refined recently, and how have they improved your
  work? How did you go about learning them?

- How have you advocated for change in your organization?
  In what ways have you impacted company policies,
  practices, or the direction of your team or department?

Add numbers wherever possible. "We decreased response times
by 50 percent by implementing a new process" is a lot more compelling than "We had our best month ever." Likewise, look for
ways to subtly pull in social proof, such as testimonials, social media
mentions, name-brand partners or collaborators, or recognition
from leaders within your company, industry organizations, or regulatory bodies. That way, those you work with don't just have to take
your word for your success—you'll show it through stamps of approval from others as well: "Our president was so pleased with the
outcome that he sent our team a thank-you note" or "We've secured a number of large sponsors for this year's event, including
Company A and Company B."

Periodically review your story bank, not only to keep the content fresh and relevant but also to ensure that you're ready to share
when it matters most. What's more, you now have a tangible, refer-
able record of your successes that you can glance at on bad days
when your impostor syndrome flares and you need a jolt of confidence. When you take a moment to internalize and savor your accomplishments, your body releases endorphins that reinforce a
feeling of competence and activity in your brain's fear center goes
down, making you more resilient to stress.

Capitalize on Casual Conversations

What have you been up to? How's that project going? What are you working on these days? The most frequent and successful visibility conversations happen during informal moments with people in your network, like when you bump into your boss's boss in the elevator or when you're chatting with an influential collaborator while waiting for others to join an online meeting.

These encounters are typically quick exchanges, so you want to deliver a short but powerful story in thirty seconds or less (usually no more than two to five sentences). Give too many details and the person may start to tune out. Dump too many accomplishments in fast succession and you look like you're trying too hard ("I did this . . . and this . . . and this . . . and this. Aren't I great?").

For example, let's say you're having lunch with a well-connected colleague who works in a different department. Instead of replying to "How are you?" with "Uh, well, I've been, you know, kind of busy . . . working on stuff. Nothing that important," you might say, "I'm part of the team rolling out our product line to a new demographic. It's an exciting growth phase, and we've already seen about 30 percent market penetration." Or . . .

- Events have been my thing lately. Our recent virtual conference had a fantastic turnout of two thousand attendees. It's been a lot of fun experimenting with gamification to keep attendees engaged.

- Customers have been keeping me busy. We introduced a loyalty program that's been huge for retention. Even [big account] is on board!

- You know how everyone has been talking about cruelty-free cosmetics lately? Well, a couple of months ago, we launched some new research into this area. Last week our VP green-lit more funding, which is really cool.

Choose details and a story that are relevant to the person you're speaking with. Say you're in a breakout group with the company's chief financial officer during a team retreat. Talk about recent cost-cutting initiatives you've put in place, not the fact that you recently took a leadership course to become a better mentor. Keep your tone on the conversational side—less jargon, more everyday language.

Beyond tactfully conveying your competence and leaving others with the impression "Hey, so-and-so really has their shit together," capitalizing on these informal moments can lead to big things for your career. One survey participant shared, "Whenever I'd periodically run into our president at meetings, I'd catch him up on what my team and I were accomplishing. Doing this consistently led him to take me under his wing. A year later, he even recommended me for a position (promotion) within his division and I got the job!"

Own Your One-on-Ones

Throughout this book, I've emphasized that your boss is your number one customer, so when you use your one-on-ones with them wisely, these discussions can not only strengthen your relationship but also boost your visibility across the organization thanks to the halo effect. When your manager thinks and speaks highly of you, other influential figures will be more likely to trust you with significant responsibilities and include you in key discussions.

It's up to you to drive these conversations by showing your

supervisor how you think (remember operational transparency from chapter 3?), how you're making *them* look good, and how you're helping them achieve *their* goals. Your boss might be too distracted or busy to notice your daily achievements because they're buried under endless meetings, firefighting urgent issues, and juggling pressures from above. They simply don't have the bandwidth to track everyone's contributions in detail, including yours. But when your boss can showcase team members like you who perform exception-ally, it helps them stand out as a leader who nurtures talent, which often translates to recognition from higher-ups and more access to resources. Your manager can also leverage your accomplishments as a conversation starter when networking with their own peers, other departments, or external partners, which often leads to collabora-tions or partnerships that benefit everyone.

Use the first part of any one-on-one to quickly and succinctly highlight "recent wins," not to simply give status updates. This could include surfacing key achievements, milestones you've hit, or other praise you and your team have received, ensuring you tie everything back to why it matters to your manager's concerns and priorities. For example:

- Before we get into our agenda, I'd like to share some good news about our Q4 goals from the recruiting front.

- I have an exciting update. We launched Project X ahead of schedule, saving us about $35,000 that could be redirected to [thing your boss cares about].

- A quick update on the pitch we talked about a few weeks ago. I met with legal to expedite the contract review, so we're on our way to closing the deal in time for you to share a revenue update at the investor meeting.

The best one-on-ones are a golden opportunity to get coaching and direction from your boss, too. Asking for help doesn't make you look helpless—if done the right way. Follow the "try 3 then ask me" rule: If you can't figure something out after trying at least three different solutions on your own, bring it up. Instead of just dropping a problem in your boss's lap (e.g., "You're so much better at X. Would you mind handling it?"), show that you've given the problem—and potential solutions—some thought: "I wanted to give you a heads-up on some challenges we're facing with distribution. We've traced it back to an issue with the scheduling system. I've tried some fixes like [options A, B, and C], but those didn't work, so I'd love to get your take. Have you encountered a similar issue before? What worked in the past?" By sharing the steps you've taken to diagnose and tackle the issue, you bring visibility to your background efforts and show that you're a proactive problem-solver.

It's also okay to be up front when you're totally stuck: "Since it's my first time handling the ad budget, I'd appreciate your tips on where to start. Could you walk me through some key points to consider? I'm eager to get moving on this and to make sure I can handle this on my own in the future." This approach shows that you're self-aware about your limitations and knowledge gaps, but that you're also willing to learn and overcome obstacles.

If there's a crisis or if your manager is visibly stressed, your one-on-one might end up being brief and transactional. It happens, but it'll be a win-win when you can relieve your boss's burden and improve your own exposure. For instance, you might say, "I've noticed you've been swamped with the client. I could help out by attending the upcoming strategy meetings and take some of the load off your plate" or "If there are any meetings coming up about this, I'd be happy to step in on your behalf. It'd be a chance for me to get more involved and bring some fresh ideas."

Show Your Strength in Meetings

Before you launch into a story based on the frameworks that follow, take a moment to read the room. Are people anxious, frustrated, or hopeful? Based on what you see and feel, choose a story that matches or constructively alters the meeting's emotional tone. For a stressed and anxious room, choose a story that is calming and solution focused. For a joyful and energetic meeting, a story that is inspiring and forward-looking will resonate well.

Problem-Action-Solution

This structure is great for project review meetings, postmortems, or strategy sessions where problem-solving is the focus. Introduce this type of story once the meeting has moved beyond general updates and when the team is diving into specific issues that have arisen or will come up. Begin by introducing the problem you were facing, emphasizing the impact it had on the company, your team, or stakeholders. For example, you could say, "More than 60 percent of customers chose to cancel or not renew their subscription, which put a lot of pressure on our sales team, lowered revenue, and introduced uncertainty." Next, describe the steps you took to solve the issue and the outcome of your actions: "I took the lead on improving customer retention. Specifically, I ran a thorough analysis of user feedback and implemented a targeted reengagement campaign." Finally, share the outcome or the result: "All of this cut our churn rate by a third, which means higher customer satisfaction and a boost in profits."

Before-After-Bridge

For meetings where the emphasis is on checking in on projects, evaluating your operations, or making your work or process better, try this structure. Bring it up when the agenda turns toward the specific project you'll be mentioning or when the discussion is more generally focused on the impact of recent changes or improvements. Start by describing the situation before you intervened. For example, one of my clients who is a coordinator at an event company shared with me: "Several weeks ago, I had to deal with what's become a persistent issue: Our photographers would arrive for a shoot only to discover there was little space to set up and no source of natural lighting. It created tension onsite and chaos for us back at the events office, since we'd have to scramble to smooth out any miscommunication." Next, describe the situation after you took action: "Since revamping our client onboarding process, we haven't received a frantic call from any of our photographers." Finally, bridge the before and after by explaining how you made the change happen: "The key change, I believe, was to have clients fill out a comprehensive questionnaire in advance along with requiring a pre-event touch-base between all parties."

Future-Focus-Forward

This structure is great for meetings that revolve around brainstorming and ideation, ideally shared at the top of the meeting so you can shape the focus for the rest of the discussion. Identify a trend or pattern you've seen in the macro environment (economic, political, etc.), your sector, or the company as a whole: "In recent years, there's been a significant shift toward making spaces more accessible for people with a wide range of physical abilities." Next, focus on how this insight presents an opportunity or a risk: "Inclusivity is important not only for ethical and legal reasons, but also because it benefits everyone we serve—our employees and patients included." Last, describe the action you took to capitalize on the trend, or share a plan to implement it moving forward: "I'd be happy to review the latest recommendations from the state and create a planning committee to address adding modifications like ramps, automatic doors, and better signage to our stores."

We-Then-Me

We live in an age when most work is a team sport, so in any meeting where you have to highlight collaboration and team effort, try "we-then-me." Talk about the group's efforts first, followed by your individual contribution: "Our new website launched last week, and the team really pulled together to get everything up on time. Carlos and Xena were very helpful in testing all the features. We're getting great feedback so far. I also took the extra step to write up a month's worth of content, so we're ahead of our production schedule." This approach shows humility, respect, and that you value collective effort, while also making sure you get credit where credit is due.

Watch for real-time reactions. Do others respond well to anecdotes and examples? That's a good sign yours will be welcomed, whereas impatience or disinterest are signs it might be better to stick with a strictly technical explanation. If you begin your story and notice that the reaction isn't as expected, don't be afraid to adjust on the fly. This might mean shortening the story, shifting focus from one aspect to another, or even pausing to ask for direct feedback before continuing. As a rule of thumb, I recommend no more than one *brief* story per meeting to make your point (or one per day if you have multiple meetings with the same people). But if you work in a more austere and task-oriented culture—or you don't get that many opportunities to speak—then one per week might be more appropriate and feasible.

COMMAND THE ROOM

Speaking up at work can enhance your status, but it's less about how often you speak and more about making sure your contributions are timely, well-prepared, and match the interests of your audience. Here's how to effectively make your mark, even when:

- **You procrastinate on speaking up.** Challenge yourself to be the second or third person to contribute. According to the primacy effect, early speakers tend to be more memorable than those who speak up later, and it'll force you to say something before your fear response kicks in.

- **You think you have nothing to add.** Ask insightful questions like "How might this decision impact X?" or "What alternatives are there?" Build on comments from others: "I think there's a consensus here about X . . ." or "Echoing what Tom said about market expansion, it's also worth considering . . ."

- **You have trouble finding the right moment to interject.** Chime in between agenda points or topics with "Before we move on, let me add . . ." or "I'm glad you brought that up. I'd like to add . . ." If you're interrupting someone more senior than you, ask for permission: "Can I add a legal perspective?" or "Is now a good time to bring up X?"

- **You tend to undercut yourself.** Instead of hedging and saying, "I might be wrong, but . . ." or "This is probably not what you're looking for . . . ," try "Here's an idea . . ." or "I believe this approach could be effective . . ." Swap qualifiers like "I'm no expert on this" or "I don't have much experience here" for phrases like "From my perspective . . ." or "Based on my understanding . . ."

- **You don't know the answer to a question.** You can defer, but explain why: "Let me do some research so I can give you the best answer possible" or "To give you the most accurate answer, I'd need to check with a few colleagues. I can touch base by Friday."

- **Your comments are ignored.** If your idea gets lost in the shuffle or inadvertently overlooked, don't let it slide. Someone else may share the same thought and get credit. Speak up after the next person goes and say something like "I didn't get feedback on X, so I wanted to know—what's your impression of what I shared?"

- **You have to disagree.** Dr. Lois Frankel, bestselling author of *Nice Girls Don't Get the Corner Office,* once told me about contrasting—stating what you are *not* saying or doing, then affirming what you *are* saying. She gave me an example of what you might say to your boss: "I don't want to contradict what you said because there's a lot of truth in it. There's one piece I want to clarify or it might lead to confusion."

- **You didn't get to share your thoughts.** Stand out by circling back: "I thought about what we discussed and after digesting it X came to mind as a possible next step." Even if it's a day or two later, you'll appear thoughtful, since most people move on to the next thing.

Beyond the Conversation

Spread the Word

You can take your visibility to the next level by circulating a monthly or quarterly update to your cross-functional partners, stakeholders, and senior leadership. Think of this like an internal newsletter: Its primary purpose is to keep everyone informed, but it also allows you to share results achieved by you, your team, or your department. This type of visibility vehicle works in large, geographically dispersed, or collaborative work cultures, where communication across departments and levels is encouraged and information exchange is necessary to keep pace with the speed of work or external demands. If you work remotely or only go into the office a few days a week, these updates serve as a proactive way to stay on people's radar and counter the "out of sight, out of mind" problem that can happen when you're not in the same physical space. Just be aware that these types of blasts may be viewed with skepticism or as unnecessary noise in highly competitive or siloed cultures or in very small teams or companies.

Before going rogue and emailing something, get approval from your manager. Pitch it as a collaborative effort with your boss and colleagues, explaining that the goal is to showcase the team's effort and progress. If possible, involve others in crafting the content (or, at the very least, signing off on it) to make sure everyone is aligned and no one is caught by surprise. If your manager says no because a regular newsletter might rock the boat too much or seems out of sync with the company culture, consider a compromise: Offer to present the same details to stakeholders in an upcoming meeting.

STEAL THIS SCRIPT

Subject: [Your Team / Department Name] Quarterly Update— [Month/Year]

Introduction: Keep it brief and friendly, like "Can you believe the year is halfway over? Here's a quick roundup of the data team's progress, insights, and standout moments from the past three months."

Highlight achievements: Bullet points or short paragraphs highlighting one to five key successes, project completions, milestones reached, or goals achieved. Give credit to the people or teams responsible, including yourself!

Offer insights: Share lessons learned, best practices, new strategies, or feedback from team members on what they've discovered.

Look ahead: Briefly outline upcoming projects, objectives, or goals. This keeps everyone aligned and excited about what's next.

Closing note: Provide a call to action to offer input or feedback about something specific, or simply end on an upbeat note: "We're looking forward to another great quarter ahead!"

Put Your Name in the Hat

I'll never forget the deep jealousy I felt when one of my colleagues was awarded a major industry honor. I wondered, "Why not me?" until I realized her secret: She had nominated herself! No matter your rank or field, the truth is that those who receive recognition are often the ones who step up and claim it for themselves. So the next time you see someone receiving acclaim and think, "I wish that were me," remember, it can be.

While it can feel weird to put yourself forward for awards, they confer credibility that can generate opportunities for you while also elevating your company's brand and providing a strong selling point for attracting new employees, business, and clients. Awards might even lead to positive media coverage for you and your organization. Read industry-specific publications, websites, and newsletters, or reach out to professional associations, your alumni network, and mentors. You can even set up a Google Alert using specific keywords like "digital marketing excellence awards [year]" or "nonprofit leadership awards in [your location]."

Beyond formal recognition, you can "nominate yourself" in other ways. For example, you might let the PR, events, or publicity team know that you're interested in representing the company on panels, at conferences, or as a guest for an internal webinar series. Perhaps you offer to write an article for your company's blog. Many of my clients have also had success hosting lunch and learns or "brown bag sessions" where they conduct an internal training session on a subject that they're passionate about.

What to Do When . . .

Someone Steals Credit for Your Work

Your personal brand is built on the recognition of your contributions and achievements, but if someone steals credit for your work, you're out of luck. If this happens to you, here are ways you can respond with poise and confidence:

- **Stay calm and set the record straight.** Chime in and say something like "It was great collaborating on the project Mary mentioned. While her team led execution, our team was responsible for strategy and we're so happy how it turned out." For an email clarification: "I'd like to jump in and clarify what Tim shared in his previous message. He did a great job sourcing the data we needed, and I compiled it into the report you see."

- **Confront carefully.** Failing to give credit might be an innocent mistake or a simple oversight. Ask before you accuse: "I noticed you took sole credit for X. Was that intentional?" or "I noticed that when you talked about the project, you said 'I' instead of 'we.' What led you to frame it that way?" You'll be making it clear you noticed, and that it wasn't right.

- **Appeal to a sense of justice and morality.** Emphasize how they'd feel if the situation was reversed: "I'm sure you've been in situations when someone represented your idea as their own, so you know it doesn't feel good. I hope you understand that's the position I'm in right now. What would you do if you were in my shoes?"

- **Set a boundary.** Make it clear your colleague's behavior is not cool: "I realize there's a lot to cover in these meetings and it's easy to leave names off the presentation. But, going forward, please make sure to credit me on the slides."

- **Protect your intellectual property.** Consider revealing your best ideas in group settings versus one-on-one. Document them in memos and emails to create a paper trail. Don't include every last detail of your idea. Something as simple as "I have a few thoughts about how to execute this" can help you keep ownership.

STEAL THESE SCRIPTS

Here are more ways to clap back when someone steals credit for your work, ranging from gentle to assertive and suitable for different contexts, including meetings and emails.

- I appreciate your interest in the idea I presented earlier. It's great to have your support and see you're on board with the direction.

- Thanks for expanding on the concept I initially proposed. I'd like to add some other thoughts based on the original framework I shared.

- Great minds think alike! When I introduced this idea, I had a similar direction in mind.

- That's along the lines of what I mentioned before about X. Happy to see it's generating conversation.

- I brought this up in yesterday's meeting. Can you elaborate on your take on it?

- Since this was part of my initial proposal, I'd love to hear the team's feedback on both of our perspectives.

- Good to hear that my original concept resonated with you. Let's make sure we stay true to the core aspects I outlined.

- I think there might be a little confusion here. This idea was something I introduced in our last brainstorm session.

- That's exactly what I was getting at when I mentioned this idea earlier.

Your Boss Excludes and Undermines You

It can be frustrating when your boss promises to loop you into important meetings but then never follows through, or when they monopolize opportunities to present work, insisting on handling all critical communications themselves. What steps can you take when your manager seems to be sabotaging your options for visibility?

- **Feign ignorance.** Approach your boss with curiosity, not passive-aggressiveness. In private mention, "I noticed I haven't been included in the last few strategy meetings. My understanding is that I should be there because [specific skill or perspective]. Could you help me understand how decisions are made regarding who attends?"

- **Get things done then and there.** After the third time Ulyssa's manager said she'd add her to important client emails but "forgot," Ulyssa tried a different approach. She began (nicely) putting her boss on the spot: "Let's set an email chain right now so it's one fewer thing on your to-do list." It worked like a charm most of the time, but every once in a while, when her manager insisted on waiting until later, Ulyssa followed up by email instead: "Thanks for meeting today. I'll look out to be added to [task/meeting] by [date]."

- **Insert yourself.** Pay close attention to upcoming deliverables and offer to draft the first version. If you're discussing an upcoming client report, you could say, "While we chat about this, I can start formatting the presentation based on our notes." This saves time and ensures you're actively involved, making it harder for your boss to cut you out later.

- **Strategically (but sparingly) carbon copy.** Ask your boss who else is involved or needs to be informed about a certain project or task. Get their agreement on this principle so that when you cc others, it seems like standard practice (which is hard to argue against). But be careful not to overdo it—pick one to three contacts to include so that your contributions are visible to others besides your boss. After sending out an email with additional cc's, gauge your manager's reaction and discuss any concerns they might have.

- **Be the bigger person.** If your boss seems to challenge every idea or contribution you attempt to make in front of others, respond with questions like "Before we get into drawbacks, can you share some reasons you think this *will* work?" or "Let's operate from the assumption that we will be successful. How does that change your point of view?" You position yourself as a proactive and positive force within the team, while highlighting to others how your boss's negativity may border on unsupportive or overly critical.

Don't wait for the "perfect moment" to "put yourself out there"—start this week and focus on capturing a story or two. While getting noticed and being praised at work feels awesome, there's an even better perk to boosting your visibility: It changes how you see *yourself*. Each time you highlight milestones to your boss or speak up in a meeting to share how you overcame a challenge, you're not just informing others—you're also reminding yourself of what you're capable of. As these wins stack up, so does your confidence. You'll start to see yourself as someone who can handle bigger projects and tougher challenges, which propels you to take on new risks and reach higher in your career than you ever imagined. Let's leverage that self-assuredness as we dive into the advancement conversation, where you'll negotiate the next steps in your career trajectory.

CHAPTER EIGHT

The Advancement Conversation

Get ahead without pissing people off

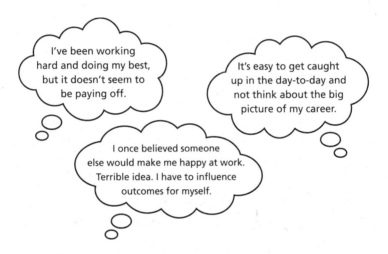

Elaine had been working hard for the previous eleven months. She was absolutely determined to get a promotion and the raise that went with it so that she could leave her obnoxious roommate behind and start the next phase of her career . . . and her life.

As a senior executive assistant at a law firm, Elaine not only managed the calendar and inbox of the partner with whom she worked but also had started a wellness committee and authored articles in law journals, which she shared in a monthly newsletter that highlighted the work and accomplishments of the support staff. On the day of her performance review, Elaine arrived nervous yet excited, confident that a promotion was in the bag after months of her boss reassuring her that she was doing a great job in her role. Seeing a close colleague in the HR department recently move up seemed to confirm that business was expanding, fueling more optimism.

It all began well enough. The managing partner complimented her initiative and gave her a small raise, but he didn't mention anything about the title change that she had been hoping for. As the meeting began to wrap up, Elaine blurted out, "I was thinking I could be chief of staff." She started to explain her rationale, but her boss cut her off.

"It's just not possible," he said. "I don't think the role you're describing is critical for the firm, and even if it were, I can't make that kind of decision on the spot. You've really caught me off guard."

"But you've said over and over that things have been going really well—you even said it just now," Elaine mumbled, simultaneously embarrassed and angry.

"Exactly. I want you to keep doing what you're doing. Listen—we can talk about it at your next review, okay?" he said awkwardly as he stood up to go. "I do think you're doing a terrific job." The meeting ended with both of them disappointed and rattled by what they had hoped (for different reasons) would be a celebratory occasion.

Elaine arrived at our session a few weeks later still feeling dejected. "So now what? Can I just quit? That's what I feel like doing."

"Do you like your job?" She nodded. "Do you still want to be chief of staff someday?" She nodded again. "Then," I said, "it's time to start having *the advancement conversation*." In the months that followed, Elaine became more strategic about her career goals using the steps you'll discover in this chapter. She sought feedback from her boss and other partners on steps she needed to take to create a chief of staff role and prepared a business case showing how it would benefit the firm. After her next review, she emailed me three words: "THEY SAID YES!"

Promotions and title changes are the most common form of advancement, but they usually happen every few years. If you pigeonhole yourself into thinking this is the only way to get ahead, you cut yourself off from opportunities to build your experience and résumé even in between promotions. Stay open-minded and consider other ways of growing your skill set and prestige—whether by pitching a stretch project; managing a bigger scope; making a lateral move to switch departments, teams, or locations; or, like Elaine, designing a completely new role that doesn't yet exist. Nevertheless, many invisible factors influence your ability to advance, from the economy to the C-suite's priorities and even timing within the company's budget cycles. Competing incentives and politics play a role, too. For example, even if your manager recognizes your potential, budget limitations or head-count restrictions imposed by HR or finance can delay your move to a higher-level role. Likewise, your department head's reluctance to lose you to another team that wants your skill set—especially if there's a history of rivalry between the managers—can also hinder your growth.

Although these factors are a reality, you don't have to be at their mercy or leave your career path to chance. In this chapter, you'll learn how to navigate the careful dance of aligning your ambitions with the often-opaque priorities of your organization. While it'd be nice if all leaders enthusiastically championed their employees' growth right off the bat, many resist change, which is why I'll show you how to turn skepticism into support—from planting the seeds of your aspirations, to crafting proposals that speak to your manager's problems, to continually advocating for yourself when faced with pushback at any (or every) stage. Don't panic if you're not your manager's favorite or you want to completely change everything about your job. There's a path to success without giving up.

It's important to note that often the advancement and money conversations occur simultaneously. For instance, when you're promoted to a leadership role, a raise is usually a part of that transition. But in many situations—when you're stepping into an interim role, for example, or you've strategically decided to gather experience in order to make a stronger case for salary negotiation in the future— the two happen separately, which is why we'll cover the money conversation on its own in the next chapter.

Match Your Wants with the Company's Needs

It's all well and good if you want to work on expanding a certain product internationally, but if your manager is focused on boosting sales locally, then your pitch might fall flat. Or, say you'd like to carve out a stretch project to improve standardized test scores for students in your district. If the school system has been dealing with administrative turnover, the new leadership might have different priorities or be hesitant to adopt new projects for a while, shoving your efforts on the back burner.

Before you make any pitch, consider the context in which you're operating and explore factors that will impact how you get what you want:

- **Where are the gaps?** Do a project inventory to determine where additional resources or expertise might be needed within your team or department. This goes beyond simply taking on extra tasks—it's about owning entire *areas* that lack attention and will drive meaningful monetary growth or save time. How could your skill set fill these voids? For example, if a lack of data analysis expertise is affecting projects across different departments, you could propose a new role focusing on analytics. Or, if there is no clear driver for a critical initiative, you might suggest a title change to "team lead" or "project manager," outlining how your leadership skills can ensure the project's success.

- **What is top of mind for your manager?** If you're having the alignment conversation (chapter 1), then you should have some clues about your boss's key objectives and what they see as most critical to the department's or company's future. Have they said things like "Our main goal is to triple our product line in the next three years," "Increasing our market share in the Middle East is a top priority," or "We have to get customer satisfaction scores up"? These are all hints on how to propose a promotion that aligns with these goals. Getting involved in these areas can strengthen your case and earn you Brownie points.

- **How well do they think you'd be able to motivate and inspire others to achieve results at a higher level?** A promotion often involves managing people, not just executing tasks, so you need to understand how your boss sees your leadership potential. Listen for praise about your teamwork, how you boost morale, or comments about your ability to work across different stakeholders. Also, notice what your manager values in a leader.

Resourcefulness, bold vision, the ability to stay calm under pressure? In your pitch, show you've already demonstrated these qualities and how you can use them in a new role. For instance, if your manager often applauds your knack for simplifying complex ideas, emphasize this strength and explain how it will help you to collaborate with nontechnical partners.

- **What is senior leadership concerned with?** Is upper management pushing for stability? Diversity and inclusion? Customer lifetime value? Their focus will trickle down to influence what initiatives get the green light—and get more money. Showing your manager that you're involved in work that matters to *their* boss can not only highlight your value and readiness for a bigger role but also make it simpler for them to sell your request up the chain of command. Even if you want to switch teams, aligning your skills and contributions with the big bosses' priorities can make you a more appealing candidate for internal transfers.

- **How does the company's fiscal calendar flow?** Be aware of the budget planning calendar, when money is tight, and how expenses are reviewed. Syncing your proposals with these cycles can increase their chances of approval. For example, if budget reviews happen in Q4, start making your case for a promotion or new project in Q3 when planning is under way. If you're interested in switching teams and a department usually gets new funding at the start of the fiscal year, prepare your case for why you'd be a valuable addition to that team and present it just before the new budget is allocated.

- **How's the economy?** Amid a downturn, your organization may freeze hiring, making it a bad time to propose growing your team with external hires. But during tough times, advocating for responsibility that streamlines processes, cuts costs, or retains good people can be a strategic approach. On the other hand, if revenue is on the upswing, there may be more openness to ideas, including stretch projects or designing roles. Listen for language that signals a willingness to invest in new directions, grow, or take chances: "diversifying our approach," "expanding our capabilities," or "scaling up."

- **What are competitors doing?** Look at their content, marketing messages, and job postings. If they're hiring, it can indicate that the industry or sector is healthy, suggesting a higher likelihood of growth opportunities at your company, too. Say you notice that a competitor is recruiting for many roles in artificial intelligence. Use this information as leverage in your promotion pitch to prove why your company needs someone like you to step into the capacity.

It's all right if what you want doesn't perfectly match up with what the organization needs or what your boss is prioritizing. We'll cover how you can make that connection soon. And even if the exact type of advancement you're seeking isn't possible today, understanding the landscape can help you strategize for the future.

STEAL THESE SCRIPTS

While a startup might promote you for launching cutting-edge products, an advertising firm may care more about account acquisition. Promotion protocols vary widely as well, from structured "calibration" cycles to ad hoc opportunities based on achievements or business needs. Use the networking skills you developed in chapter 6 to talk to people who have advanced on a pathway similar to the one you imagine for yourself or who work in the department or area you're interested in. Choose from these questions:

- How does the promotion process work here? Is it tied to set periods or more fluid? Is there a standard tenure required?

- What key skills and experiences helped you advance? How did you stand out in your role and demonstrate your value?

- How would you suggest going about being selected for a project like X?

- Did you have a mentor or sponsor who helped guide your career? If so, how did they support you?

- How did you prepare to advocate for yourself? Is there anything you didn't say or do that you wish you had said or done?

- In the case of changing departments, what does the approval process look like? Who has to be involved?

- Is there room in our organization for customizing your role based on your personal strengths or interests? How does that work?

- What challenges or obstacles have you faced with trying to get ahead here? How did you overcome them?

- When you were promoted, did you play a role in training your successor or organizing your transition? How was that perceived by management?

Get Your Boss On Board

The advancement conversation isn't a quick sidebar in your annual review. It's a long game—and can last anywhere from three to six months in a small or midsize company to a year (or more!) if you work in a company or an industry with slower career progression or if you're looking to advance into a higher-stakes role. You want your boss to hear about your goals early on in the proces so that they become more and more familiar with them and also increase the likelihood that they will support them. This doesn't mean you have to talk about your ambitions every day (that would be annoying), but it does mean that you should be intentional about bringing them up gently and periodically.

Seed your aspirations using positive language that not only feels warm and appreciative but uses a future-oriented focus. Here are a few suggestions for when to make your pitch:

- **During a one-on-one.** Say your boss shares an update about a new pharmaceutical the broader team is developing. Respond with enthusiasm: "Great to hear that we're getting into the therapeutics space. How are we navigating the regulatory aspect? I see myself contributing on the compliance side in the future."

- **After you complete a project**. Try something like "I'm thrilled with how the exhibit turned out. Leading the construction was really rewarding. It's given me a taste of what a more senior role could be like, especially strategic planning. I'd love to get more opportunities like this as I prepare to move into leadership."

- **When you've received positive feedback**. Say more than "thank you": "I appreciate the kind words about the employee rewards program. I'm actually looking to expand it even further. I'd love to take on more responsibilities that fit with [a bigger role]."

- **In casual conversation**. Having lunch or coffee with your boss or a more senior colleague? Let them in on your plans: "I've always found the work your department does to be fascinating. How did you get started in that area? I'm curious because it's a direction I've started exploring myself."

How does your manager respond to your bids? Do they lean in with curiosity and interest or brush you off? Are they giving you feedback or specific compliments that focus on your future potential: "Great job with X. Focusing on Y could really prepare you for [new responsibility]"? Are you being assigned to influential projects or invited to contribute in bigger and bigger ways? Don't rush to conclusions if your boss isn't immediately enthusiastic. Adjust how frequently or in what settings you mention your intentions or experiment with different phrasing. Still not getting much of a response after a few more tries? Maybe your boss is preoccupied. Maybe they're oblivious. Don't just abandon your efforts—move on to having a more explicit conversation. If your boss shoots down your ideas (e.g., "Now's not the right time" or "I need you where you are"), ask for specifics: "Can you help me understand what's standing in the way?" or "What can I work on to be better prepared for X?" That may be enough to clear the logjam, but if not, we'll deal with how to react when your boss objects, pushes back, or completely stalls you throughout the rest of this chapter.

Put Your Cards on the Table

The next step is to agree on where you're going—and get clarity on what it'll take to get to a higher level. Different skills? More experience? A better understanding of the organization? Ideally, this conversation gives you a checklist of sorts, so you know what areas to focus on and how to present your case when the time arrives. But it can also reveal objections you have to overcome.

Ahead of your next one-on-one, email your boss and say you'd like to discuss your development. You don't have to give all the details, but do give a heads-up that you want to have a bigger-picture discussion so they're not surprised. Draw on the thinking you did earlier and hint at how your goals are beneficial and relevant to your manager or the company as a whole. Present this discussion in one of the following ways:

- **Tie it to organizational timing.** As we look ahead to [the next quarter, fiscal year end, etc.], I'd like to get your insights on how I can grow within our team and the company. It's important to me that my role evolves in a way that supports [team's mission / key project / your boss's priority].

- **Connect it to a recent achievement.** I've been reflecting on my recent work, particularly [accomplishment], and it got me thinking about my future. Could we set aside time to discuss my role and how I can add more value, specifically around [area]? I have some ideas for what this could look like and I'm eager to get your input.

- **Ground it in an industry shift.** Given the shift toward [industry trend / competitor move / market change], we need to stay a step ahead. I've been thinking about how I could take on [ask] to respond to this and make sure we're at the forefront of these changes.

If your boss seems to be open to what you're proposing, great! But even if they're neutral or reluctant at this stage, being inquisitive and consultative will raise your chances of eventually getting buy-in and may reveal key details that validate your assumptions about how what you're gunning for does or does not match your boss's or the organization's priorities. Maybe they're not convinced you're ready, or perhaps they're worried about the extra work it'll create for them. They might be concerned about setting a precedent that leads to a flood of similar requests they can't honor. Ask questions like the following to get as many specifics as possible about what your manager needs to see and by when:

- What milestones or metrics would show I'm ready for [desired role]? I'd like to have clear targets to aim for.

- What specific skills or experiences do you feel would prepare me to take on [larger function]? Are there particular areas you think I need to develop further?

- Do we have a typical timeline or career progression path for moving into [new responsibilities]? I'd like to set realistic goals for myself based on that.

- Are there any internal hurdles or political dynamics that I need to be aware of?

- Who else needs to be on board with the decision to advance me to [role]? If you have any suggestions about reaching out to them—or if you're willing to make a direct introduction—I'd appreciate it.

If there's a mismatch between your boss's criteria and your network's feedback, give more weight to the opinions of those who have the most sway over your career or projects, even if that includes leaders besides your manager. Maybe colleagues have shared that getting a special certification helped them stand out, but your boss says they believe hands-on experience, not more education, is key to driving a certain project in the future. If your direct supervisor controls the assignments that could lead to a promotion, their preference should guide your actions. But if your company follows recommendations from a panel or senior leadership team that values continuous education, pursuing that special certification might serve you better in the long term. Whatever you do, don't name-drop people in your network with whom you've spoken—unless you have a very open and transparent relationship with your boss and you work in a highly collaborative culture. Otherwise, the revelation of those details could make your boss feel left out and create tension. Discuss any discrepancies with a mentor or trusted advisor within the organization to get a second opinion.

STEAL THESE SCRIPTS

In the course of sharing your intentions to advance, your manager may throw up roadblocks that could alter your game plan or lengthen your timeline. Don't give up, though. Here's what to do instead when your boss . . .

Gives you vague metrics to aim for

Request examples where similar goals have been met: "When you say taking initiative is important, what's a time when someone demonstrated the kind of success you're looking for? What specific actions did they take?" Switch to binary or either/or questions: "Are you suggesting I focus on making sure we're complying with current standards, or would you prefer I prepare for upcoming regulatory changes?"

Won't commit to a timeline

The reasons might not be obvious from the outside looking in, so gently probe to understand more: "I know a lot is in flux at the moment. Are there external factors that influence how we're thinking about project assignments?" or "Since my last review was positive, I'm trying to understand the hesitancy. Am I missing something?"

Says you have to wait for the next cycle

Do some digging to understand limitations: "Are there a set number of promotions available each cycle?" You could also propose an interim review: "Given that the next cycle is far off, could we do an interim check-in to discuss my progress on the areas we've identified? That way, I can make sure I'm on track and make adjustments as needed."

Says advancement isn't possible, even though you're doing well

We'll talk soon about what to do when you're rejected or totally hit a dead end, but start by negotiating an alternative. Offer an option that would both serve as evidence of your capability and be a great résumé builder should you decide it's actually wiser to leave: "I understand that a formal promotion isn't an option right now. Instead, could we consider having me temporarily lead the social media team?"

Present Your Game Plan

Whether putting your cards on the table goes well or not, put together a simple document or slide deck within one to six weeks that outlines the action steps you'll take. If the discussion is decently positive and your boss seems at least somewhat receptive, use this document to walk them through your plans in real time. If the conversation doesn't yield the support you hoped for, keep this plan as a personal record. It's useful to have a well-thought-out strategy ready should an unexpected opportunity arise, even if you don't share it with your boss right away.

Highlight how the tasks you're devoting time to meet these criteria. Don't just zero in on what a new opportunity or more power would do or mean for you (e.g., moving to a new team gets you away from your jerk colleague, or a larger scope—and the salary that goes along with it—will allow you to send your kids to private school). Help your boss envision the benefits they can expect, a concept borrowed from marketing called future pacing: "Having additional head count means we can scale client acquisition an extra 20 percent over the next six months" or "Changing my title to X would enable me to have more clout with our customers and build our book of business in this new sector." Here's a sample pitch:

> Hey [Boss], thanks again for the helpful discussion about my goals to [desired position / role / responsibilities]. I've put together a game plan that covers the areas for development we discussed.
>
> My goal is to [insert goal—lead a small project team, increase sales by X percent, etc.] in the next [insert time frame—three to six months, year, etc.]. I see this not only helping me to meet my personal goals to [your aspiration] but also helping the team/company [add potential benefits and possible impact].
>
> I know that I'll also need to develop [key skills and competencies]. In terms of actions to help me get there, here's what I've planned:
>
> - For training, I'm looking at [list courses/workshops].
>
> - To gain hands-on experience, I plan to [name projects or stretch assignments].
>
> - I'll seek guidance from [mention mentor or someone you'll network with].
>
> Before I go any further, I'd love to get your input. Are there areas you think I should adjust or other elements you believe I should consider?

Request that you and your manager earmark one one-on-one each month or quarter to touch base on your progress and goals. In between these meetings, document successes and key learnings in your story bank (chapter 7), detailing how they map to the criteria outlined in your plan: "We both agreed cross-functional influence is a skill I need to be ready for [new responsibility]. I've been coordinating email campaign dates and messaging with sales—and we haven't missed a mailing since. Sally, your peer on the business development side, said the support has been invaluable." Consistent checkpoints also give you the opportunity to reassess and adjust, which lessens the likelihood that unexpected organizational shifts or uncontrollable roadblocks take you by surprise or stymie your progress.

STEAL THESE SCRIPTS

At any point in the process, you need to be prepared to answer potential questions or concerns like the following that your boss might have about your readiness or the feasibility of your advancement.

I don't think your timeline is doable.

I'm open to adjusting the plan, but I do want to emphasize how important [specific goal] is to my growth and satisfaction. What if we find a middle ground where [compromise], which allows me to grow while addressing your concerns?

Do you really think you can handle everything [role] will throw at you?

That's a fair question. I've pushed myself in [specific projects or tasks] and I feel like I've grown a lot from those experiences. Sure, there are going to be new challenges, but I'm ready to tackle them head-on.

Handling [specific skill or responsibility] is a big part of [role]. Are you up for that?

Yes, I've been really focusing on that area lately. I took a course in [skill] and have been applying it regularly, especially in [task]. I'm still polishing it, but I'm excited to bring these skills to the new role and expand them.

Don't you think you should brush up on [skill] before taking on [new responsibility]?

There's always room to grow. I've got a solid base in [specific area], but I'm actively working on [advanced skill]. I'm lining up some [resources] to make sure I'm covering all the bases.

It's a different ball game dealing with [new team / stakeholders]. How do you think you'll fit in?

I've given this some thought. I plan to start by really listening and getting to know everyone's perspectives. I've always believed in teamwork and open communication, and I think that's going to help me find my place.

[Role] can be pretty high-pressure. How will you handle that?

I've had a taste of pressure in [specific situations], and I've found that staying organized and keeping cool work for me. I also believe in reaching out when I need help.

Press the Matter

Despite your best efforts to keep the advancement conversation on track and navigate objections using what we've covered in this chapter so far, your boss may still string you along, stall, or otherwise block your path. Here's what to do when your boss . . .

Says the company's not doing well

Possible causes: Maybe issues with market saturation, increased competition, or the supply chain are affecting your team's budget for new projects or promotions. Changes in consumer behavior, the loss of a major customer, or poor management decisions can impact the company's finances as well.

How to handle it:

- **Fill the vacuum.** During hard times, ask yourself, "How can I make this situation work *for me* instead of *against me?*" Align your efforts with the company's new priorities, which probably include increasing efficiency, improving profitability, maintaining stability, and preserving their reputation. That may mean, for example, jettisoning innovation projects and focusing on essential operations until further notice.

- **Look for quick wins.** For example, you could find a cheaper way to source materials, collaborate with another department to conserve resources, implement automation to streamline a process, or develop a campaign to boost repeat purchases. Leverage these successes to negotiate for your future: "I'm happy to continue taking on X, as long as there is a commitment to revisit my scope down the road" or "I can absolutely help with X, but my ultimate goal is to go in Y direction. When do you think this can happen?"

Is distracted by urgent issues

Possible causes: Perhaps your manager is consumed by a demanding, mission-critical project. They might be dealing with personnel problems, coordinating a restructuring, a merger, or an acquisition, or even battling health issues. Any of these situations could make your advancement conversation an afterthought.

How to handle it:

- **Minimize their workload.** If your boss cancels your development plan touch-bases, don't say, "No problem!" and move on. Reschedule instead: "I'll grab a time in a few weeks once things settle down with [project]." Consider shifting part of the conversation to email or a shared document: "I know your time is tight, so to make things easier, I'll track updates toward [key experience] here. That way you can give feedback and updates on any changes as it suits your schedule."

- **Make use of brief moments.** If you bump into your boss in a common area or have a few minutes before others join a call, you might say, "I know you've been swamped, but I wanted to quickly mention I've made a lot of progress on [task]." When delivering a report, for example, include a section or footnote that highlights actions taken toward the development goals you've discussed, reminding your boss of the ongoing conversation in a subtle way.

Claims, "Yeah, yeah, everything's being approved," yet nothing seems to be happening

Possible causes: In many organizations, especially larger ones, there may be multiple layers of approvals, which slow the process. Your boss might believe that since you are already performing at a higher level, the formal recognition can wait or perhaps they overpromised without having the actual authority or resources to grant your request.

How to handle it:

- **Clarify the process.** Get the details: "What stages are left before the promotion is finalized? That will help me manage my expectations and plan accordingly" or "Can you share who ultimately gives the green light for me to join [project team]? I'd like to understand how the approval flows."

- **Offer to assist.** Ask your manager if there's anything you can do to help them navigate bureaucratic hurdles: "I understand that these things can sometimes be held up by missing information or paperwork. Would it help if I compile or organize some of the required documents? Or perhaps I can draft a summary of my contributions and initiatives that justify this title change for the review committee?"

Stonewalls you for no apparent reason

Possible causes: You may hit a dead end at any or all steps in the advancement conversation because of reasons we've already discussed—

resource constraints, organizational changes, your boss's lack of authority, and more. But some managers may obstruct your progress
because of their own insecurities, fear of competition, and personal
biases.

How to handle it:

- **Consult HR.** Log details about times you've discussed
  advancement with your manager but no clear action plan
  was provided or when criteria seemed to shift or
  contradict. Approach HR to clarify company policies on
  promotions and career development: "Could we review
  the steps I've taken to determine if there's a pattern or
  misunderstanding I'm not seeing?," "Beyond speaking
  with my boss, are there other internal advocacy channels
  I should consider?," or "I've noticed some inconsistencies
  in feedback regarding my readiness for X. Could you
  share how I can get a clearer assessment of what's
  needed for me to progress?"

- **Find a sponsor.** In a moment, we'll talk about leveraging
  others' input to sway your boss, but if your manager can't or
  won't support you, you have to look for other powerful
  advocates. Seek out influential individuals in your reporting
  line, leaders of departments, or executives who have a track
  record of speaking up on behalf of others and are known for
  their supportive nature. Once you use the skills and steps in
  chapter 6 to build a strong connection over the course of
  several months, directly ask if they'd be willing to endorse
  you for a high-profile project, write a recommendation to
  the promotion panel, or help you transition to another
  team.

Beyond the Conversation

Ask Others to Put in a Good Word

It's one thing for you to assert your readiness to advance, but it's far more compelling when others with power vouch for your abilities and potential. If you've been using social proof as part of your story bank (chapter 7), now's the moment to double down on the recognition you've received from others. Perhaps you bring social media mentions to one or more of your advancement conversations or, even better, ask someone to check in with or write to your boss on your behalf. Having multiple advocates creates "surround sound" that amplifies your importance and can convince decision-makers who might be hesitant if only hearing your side.

For instance, you might say to a mentor or senior colleague, "I've been thinking a lot about my next steps in the company and feel ready to take on more responsibility. If it comes up in conversation, I'd love it if you could share your thoughts on my contributions with [decision-maker]. Your opinion carries a lot of weight, and I think it could be helpful." If someone gives you a meaningful compliment, see if they'll forward it to your boss by asking, "I'm really glad to hear you think my work on [task] was exceptional. I'm looking to progress to [specific role] in the coming months and your feedback means a lot. Would you mind mentioning this to [my boss] next time you talk with them?"

You can also try to recruit peer support: "I wanted to thank you again for the great teamwork on [recent project]. I'm planning to discuss my career path with my manager soon. If it's not too much to ask, would you be willing to share your positive experience about working together with them?"

Make Yourself Dispensable

Humans are innately loss averse, so when you say you'd like to move up or into a different role, your boss's reaction might be "But who will do your current job?!" The thought of replacing you, and possibly facing worse work quality or lower productivity during the transition, can trigger resistance. So in parallel with the other parts of the advancement conversation, consider how you'll hand off certain tasks or duties (or your entire position!) when the time comes. Yes, many companies and teams are agile enough to hire a replacement or backfill a role pretty easily. But being ready to alleviate this burden for your boss can expedite your advancement and leave a long-lasting positive impression. At the same time, you want to approach the situation delicately. Suggesting someone take over a project could be perceived as a lack of commitment or as violating the hierarchy if you're not careful.

As we touched on earlier in this chapter, conversations with your network can help you suss out if you need to identify an official successor, whether it's enough to have some general suggestions about how to reallocate your responsibilities, or whether to stay away from the topic completely. If, based on the cultural signals, you decide to proceed, pay attention to who on your team takes initiative, consistently produces high-quality results, and has skills and abilities that complement your own. If the person is your direct report, you can ask them straight-out about their career goals, but feel out your peers' level of interest and bandwidth with questions like:

- How's your workload these days? I've seen you've been juggling X and Y. Is it manageable or are you swamped?

- Your work on [task] was fantastic. Have you ever thought about doing more in that area?

- I remember you mentioned wanting to gain more experience in [area]. I have some tasks that might give you exactly that. Want to sit down and talk about it?

- I could use your insight on [task] since I know you've done something similar before. Do you have time to help me out a bit?

When the topic comes up with your boss, pose it as a question: "Based on her recent work, I think Emily could be a great fit for stepping into my role with [project]. What are your thoughts on starting to involve her more as I transition to [new area]?" To avoid sounding presumptuous, use phrases like "potential candidate" or "possible prospect" rather than making definitive statements about who should replace you. If you're in an individual contributor role, think about ways to automate parts of your workflow to be less labor intensive and free up your time to focus elsewhere, or bring on contractors to support certain pieces of the work.

What to Do When . . .

Your Boss Plays Favorites

It's demoralizing to be passed over for opportunities your boss regularly offers to your peers. If you're implementing the steps from visibility and networking, then the good news is you have champions in your corner to counterbalance your manager's preference for

other team members, but it still takes work to keep your head up.
Here's how to keep going:

- **Analyze their interactions.** Is the favored employee always
  one step ahead in planning—or perhaps they have a
  knack for problem-solving on the fly? Are they providing
  bold ideas, supporting others' proposals, or perhaps
  steering conversations to solutions? Understanding the
  substance of their contributions and the style of their
  communication can give you cues on how to craft your
  own inputs.

- **Befriend the chosen one.** When Daniel's colleague Cindy
  was tapped to attend an industry conference over him,
  he opted for professionalism instead of pettiness. He
  introduced Cindy to key clients by email before she left
  and scheduled lunch when she came back to discuss
  what she had learned and to follow up on potential
  assignments. Having a strong relationship with "the
  golden child" could also put you in a more favorable
  light.

- **Ask to receive.** Make your ambitions known and ask what
  more you can do to position yourself for special projects:
  "The project Austin has been assigned to is the type of
  work I'd like to be doing. What can I do to set myself up
  to be selected for similar assignments in the near future?"

- **Compare yourself.** Highlight how you plug gaps or
  complement the skills and strengths of the favorite.
  During a team meeting you might chime in, "Pejman
  has a knack for knowing what the client wants. When

22922522522522522252292225229222522922252292225229229225225229229225229229225

we team up, I find that my background in economics helps add depth to our pitches." Or in a one-on-one with your manager, perhaps you share, "I noticed that Greyson excels in the initial creative brainstorming. I'm then able to take those big ideas and distill them into actionable steps, which is a skill set we need on [project]."

You Want to Change Everything

Quitting isn't the only option (although we'll discuss how to do it well in chapter 10!). There's often less dramatic and more rewarding paths to find satisfaction. Here's how to tailor your workday to include more of what you enjoy—a process known as job crafting—without immediately upending everything:

- **Look back to go forward.** Hayley, a pension fund performance manager, felt torn. She loved her company and colleagues, but knew she didn't want her boss's job—not today, or ever. To cut through her confusion, I asked her to recall her past five to seven roles. What did she like the most? The least? What was most important to her in her career right now? Through this exercise, it became clear her passion had evolved from finances to mentoring and coaching other female employees.

- **Remix your role.** Consider how you might change or evolve the nature or number of your responsibilities (task crafting). For instance, you might restructure your schedule to dedicate certain parts of the week to a creative project you enjoy or perhaps you start spending more time on research duties instead of client-facing activities. Hayley was able to delegate aspects of reporting to a staff member, which then freed her up to accept invitations to speak at new-hire onboarding events.

- **Shape your relationships.** Relational crafting is all about altering who you interact with, and how. As time went on, Hayley began to see the potential to carve out a role offering leadership coaching to the firm's different teams. Using her networking skills, she began intentionally chatting with her Employee Engagement colleagues in common areas like the cafeteria, which allowed her to express her interests casually. That led to them reaching out to her for consultation on coaching programs they were considering and Hayley getting invited to executive meetings that discussed the topic as well.

- **Update your identity.** The last aspect of job crafting is cognitive crafting, or shifting how you perceive your work and the meaning behind it. Perhaps you're an administrative assistant who sees her job as an opportunity to help people and make their lives easier, not just proofread documents. Think about your job description in new ways that highlight the most fulfilling aspects. Hayley reframed her role from being just about performance metrics to being about empowering and uplifting future leaders within the firm.

- **Use your job as a testing ground.** Despite Hayley's efforts, it became clear that senior management was going to be slow to decide whether to formalize a coaching program within the company. Undeterred, Hayley used the opportunity to experiment with different leadership frameworks and philosophies that could be applied both within her current role and in her own business one day, which kept her motivated and served her future endeavors. Consider how you might look for low-risk ways to experiment with the change you want to make before going all in. Perhaps you shadow someone to see what their day is like. Maybe you take a consulting project on the side or sign up for a course to confirm that you want to further pursue an interest.

You might not be itching to move up or out of your current role yet, and that's totally fine. But don't think you have to put off having the advancement conversation. Start now so that you're prepared when the time comes to make your case. Challenge yourself to chat with one person in your company who can give you the lowdown on how to *really* get ahead and then begin to position yourself to meet critical needs that help fulfill your own, your boss's, and the company's objectives. While getting a promotion or being tapped for an important project is pretty great, remember that advancement comes in all shapes and sizes. The best part for most people? The bigger paycheck that should come with it! In the next chapter, we'll get into the money conversation, turning those uncomfortable salary talks into successful negotiations.

CHAPTER NINE

The Money Conversation

Ask for (and get) the compensation you deserve

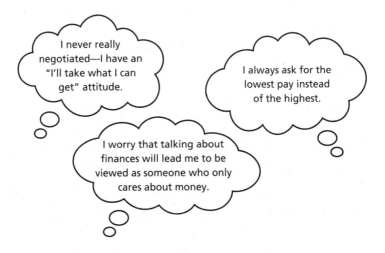

I never really negotiated—I have an "I'll take what I can get" attitude.

I always ask for the lowest pay instead of the highest.

I worry that talking about finances will lead me to be viewed as someone who only cares about money.

As the head of customer enablement at a tech company, Esadowa led a team of more than two hundred people working across Tokyo, Mumbai, and New York. His most recent win was presenting to the company's biggest account, who then agreed to roll out the company's project tracking software to 3,500 more employees in their Asia-Pacific offices, representing millions of dollars in annual revenue. His manager, Rene, the VP of operations, was ecstatic, but even more than that, Esadowa began to see himself taking a more active role in upselling their current customers.

His next one-on-one with Rene was their quarterly career chat about Esadowa's future. "So, do you want to be VP of customer success? I think you're ready for it." Esadowa was intrigued, so after work that day he started googling job descriptions and salaries for VPs of customer success. In his search, he stumbled across data showing that his current compensation was less than half of what was typical for a head of customer enablement with his level of experience. "That can't be right," he thought and texted a college friend who was now an executive recruiter. She didn't think Esadowa was making 50 percent less than his peers, but she was confident he was undercompensated by about 30 percent.

Esadowa spent the next few days in a daze—should he look for a new job? He and his husband wanted to adopt a child, so was now really the right time to make a move? "If I were being paid well, I don't think I'd be thinking about leaving," he told me.

"How have you approached *the money conversation* with Rene? Have you ever had a frank talk about your salary, stock options, or other benefits?" I asked.

Esadowa thought about it for a second. "Nope. When I joined the company fresh out of college, there was a recession and I felt grateful to land a job. Plus, I had no experience in customer success. They were taking a chance on me. I didn't think I had any room for negotiation."

After that, there was always some justification for why it was never the right time to bring up money—the company's annual investor meeting was just around the corner, they were going public, or they were knee-deep in road-map planning. "I've always thought of myself as a team player," Esadowa said, "so I've just taken what they offered me. I never wanted to make a fool of myself were they to say, 'Sorry, we can't—or won't—pay you more.'" But now Esadowa's resentment was building. When he was in meetings with his peers from other functions, he'd wonder *how much are they making?*

Even though the stigma around openly discussing compensation is diminishing, decades of secrecy and discomfort have left many professionals feeling unprepared and ill-equipped to accurately gauge their worth. That changes now. In this chapter, you'll discover not only how to research market rates and put together a strategic business case about why you're entitled to more, but also how to deliver your justification confidently using various leverage points (seniority, skill level, etc.). There's a fine line between asserting your worth and appearing aggressive, so you'll also sharpen your skills at navigating emotional undercurrents with your boss, including responding tactfully to pushback and lowball offers.

In the last chapter, we talked about how advancement and money conversations often go hand in hand. But in certain situations you'll want to discuss compensation without advancement being the primary factor. Scope creep is a classic example—when your role gradually yet significantly expands to permanently involve higher-level tasks or skills that weren't part of your original job description. Big events within the company, like a new round of financing, undergoing a sale, or experiencing a major reorganization, can also drastically alter the organizational landscape—and potentially your workload or the complexity of your responsibilities—to the point where it makes sense to reassess your compensation, even in the absence of formal promotion or advancement.

Perhaps more important, you could miss out on as much as $600,000 to $1 million in earnings and retirement savings over your lifetime. Because of compounding, a successful negotiation even for a small annual increase can be significant. For instance, take a thirty-five-year-old making an average U.S. salary of

$64,000. If they negotiate a nominal 4 percent increase each year until they turn fifty-five, they'd increase their earnings 119 percent to more than $140,000 annually. So ask yourself, "What would I do with all that extra money? What could that mean for my comfort, happiness, and sense of security—and that of my family?"

"I Can Have Money or Meaning, Not Both"

"For years, I've focused on what we've been able to do for our students versus what I was earning," a consultant at an education advocacy organization told me. "I worry I'll be seen as a squeaky wheel if I ask for more money." Many professionals, especially those in helping and creative professions or the nonprofit world, are often taught that you can earn a handsome salary *or* do meaningful work. This kind of black-and-white thinking isn't true and sets you up for long-term professional frustration.

Consider an alternative: Meaning is great, but meaning *plus* money is even better. When you're paid fairly, you're more dedicated to doing good work, and everyone wins. Your boss, leaders, colleagues, and customers all benefit from your increased dedication and capacity, since studies show that employees who are satisfied with their pay are more likely to be content with their jobs and committed to their organizations. And from a practical perspective, it's often cheaper and easier for the company to give you more money than it is to hire someone new, which can be time-consuming, expensive, and uncertain.

"I'm Afraid to Say or Do the Wrong Thing"

How could I ever look my boss in the eye again if I'm turned down? How would I deal with continuing to work here knowing that I'm undervalued? And perhaps most important, *What would the rejection mean about me and the worth of my work?* The desire to shield yourself from painful emotions like embarrassment and shame creates pressure to find a foolproof script when you want a raise. You think, "If I just had the right words or formula, I'd be golden."

The truth is that there's no perfect phrasing that if delivered in *just the right way* will guarantee success. Even if you don't secure a raise on your first attempt, you've achieved two crucial things: First, you've gained experience and the confidence that comes from trying, which is invaluable. Second, you've gathered critical data about your company's compensation processes, like which departments or roles are being prioritized and how your boss or others perceive your contributions, all of which can help you make a stronger case on your next attempt.

"I'll Face Backlash"

The fear of retaliation and coming off as greedy, ungrateful, or confrontational is especially real for women, minorities, and people of color, who are perceived as "less nice" and more "difficult" and "demanding" than their white male counterparts when they ask for more. While achieving full pay equity and dismantling long-standing biases in the workplace will take time, you can start advocating for yourself and others right now. For example, if team-wide compensation changes come up during a meeting, try to get to the bottom of them: "How did we arrive at these figures, and how often are they reviewed to ensure they're fair?" In a town hall with executives, ask a respectful but direct question like "What steps are being taken to audit and address any potential pay disparities?" You can also mentor junior employees and guide them on how to bring up salary with their own superiors. Or openly discuss your compensation with co-workers (we'll discuss how to do this without making it weird in a bit).

Besides, wouldn't it be worse to avoid speaking up and not know what was possible? As one female communications manager told me, "I worked to the point of burnout and threatened to quit, but was then offered a $25,000 raise to stay. I was happy, but also angry because they obviously could have paid me more and hadn't done it. Now I'm better at advocating for myself, keeping receipts on my accomplishments, and not waiting until the point of no return to have a conversation with my boss."

"Fuck You, Pay Me"

When I was a brand-new business owner, I watched a Creative-Mornings talk by designer Mike Monteiro called "Fuck You, Pay Me," inspired by Ray Liotta's classic monologue in the movie *Goodfellas*, when Liotta's character, mobster Henry Hill, talks about getting what he's owed. He says, "Business bad? Fuck you, pay me. Oh, you had a fire? Fuck you, pay me. Place got hit by lightning, huh? Fuck you, pay me." While I wouldn't recommend cursing out your boss, there's something to be said for an unapologetic attitude toward being fairly compensated. So the next time you're gearing up for that all-important money conversation, channel a bit of Liotta's unwaver-ing conviction (but maybe leave the mob attitude at the door).

Do Your Homework

There may never be a "good" time for a money conversation, but a little organizational awareness will go a long way toward increas-ing your chances of success. Here are some ways to gauge the fi-nancial health of your company and judge whether it's the right time to make an ask:

- **Check your company's financial statements.** Consistent upward trends in earnings reports and strong profit margins usually indicate that the company is growing and potentially more open to salary increases. Look for language like "exceeded expectations" or "record-breaking quarter." Mentions of budget cuts, cost reductions, or austerity measures? Not great signs.

- **Pay attention to new business announcements.** Has your organization recently undertaken major new partnerships or big, long-term contracts, especially those that open new markets or significant revenue streams? Even better if they're with industry leaders or governmental agencies (which tend to be more stable).

- **Read the industry tea leaves.** See if there's news showing that your company is outperforming competitors in key areas like market share, innovation, or customer satisfaction. Be cautious if your organization (or your industry as a whole) is facing headwinds like regulatory

challenges, declining demand, or disruptive technology
that the business is struggling to adapt to.

- **Snoop job listings.** If your organization is actively hiring, it
may be a sign that times are good and management
could potentially afford to give raises. If you see a sudden
slowdown or hiring is limited to replacing essential
personnel or for very specific, short-term projects only,
that may not bode as well.

- **Consider market conditions.** Google discussions about
talent shortages in your field. Look for articles or reports
that highlight a "skills gap" in your area of expertise.
Make note of competitors that are increasing salaries or
benefits to retain talent in roles similar to yours. All of
this can signify that you're in high demand and may
mean you can command a bigger percentage increase.

The more senior you are, the better your insight into the company's financials may be, given your exposure to executive-level discussions, which allows you to time your request more appropriately. Likewise, if you're in a leadership role, your understanding of compensation structures (as someone who might set them for others) can help you craft a compelling argument for your own raise by showing how you meet or exceed predetermined benchmarks. Being in a high-demand industry or having sought-after skills often means you're regularly contacted by recruiters. Not only does this interest give you up-to-date market intelligence about salaries but it can also be carefully leveraged to suggest you deserve competitive compensation from your current employer.

Once you've sifted through the signals, you might determine that it's not the best time to ask for a raise. You're not admitting defeat; rather, you're playing the long game, understanding the landscape, and making a smart, calculated move. The right time will come, and when it does, you'll be more than ready to speak up.

Build Your Business Case

Your boss needs concrete numbers and metrics to justify *to their superiors* that investing in you would yield a positive return. Assuming that you've decided, based on the criteria above, that it's a good enough time to have the money conversation, you then have to do some crucial prep work to show that (1) you're already a valuable contributor and (2) the company could reap potential upside from giving you more moola.

Before you ever set foot in your boss's office, revisit your story bank (chapter 7) and pull out some of the most meaningful accomplishments, focusing on the ones that quantify the value you bring to the table. If it's early in your career, include metrics around your contributions to projects (task completion rates, quality scores, process improvement measurements), your ability to meet or exceed performance targets, and any additional responsibilities you've taken on. If you're in a mid-level role, gather data around your team's performance (productivity, engagement scores, project delivery timelines), how you've executed against departmental goals, and how you've kept things running efficiently (compliance rates, customer retention, etc.). As a senior leader, your justification for a raise may revolve around revenue growth, cost savings, profit margins, market share, or your ability to build a pipeline of high-potential talent.

If you're struggling to assign specific numbers to your actions, consider one or more of these work-arounds:

- **Assign a range.** Unsure about exactly how many clients you served or the number of deliverables you touched? Estimate using a range: "Since January, I've saved the operations team between sixty and ninety hours."

- **Consider the frequency.** How often did you do a particular task? Daily? Weekly? Monthly? For example: "I've assumed the responsibility of troubleshooting our help desk queue twice a day for the last six months."

- **Compare and contrast.** Peg your outcomes against those of your peers, competitors, or industry standards: "I directed a flash sale email campaign that produced a 40 percent open rate, which is 30 percent above industry average."

- **Think qualitatively.** No numbers to point to whatsoever? Put together a social proof document with impressive customer testimonials or devise mini case studies to convey your impact.

Focus not only on the ROI from your *past* contributions but also on the *potential* ROI you can offer going forward if compensated for it. Use data from similar projects within your company or ones that you've worked on directly. For example, if a previous outreach effort increased donations by 15 percent, use this as a baseline for what you could achieve. You can also get projections to build your case using the social capital you built in chapter 6 through the networking conversation. Perhaps you ask someone in sales for insights into customer acquisition costs. A contact in finance could give you specifics on profit margins and budget allocation, while someone on the service delivery side could provide customer satisfaction metrics. Just as it's fine to offer a range for your past results, it's also fine to offer a range of projections: "Conservatively, Project X could increase re-signs by 10 percent, leading to an estimated revenue increase of \$Y. Optimistically, we could see up to a 20 percent increase, generating \$Z additional revenue."

I suggest pulling your business case together into a document or slide deck—similar to the way you drafted your plan in the advancement conversation—incorporating easy-to-follow headers (e.g., Track Record, Results, Future Growth, Projected ROI), skimmable bullets, and visuals (pie chart, before-and-after comparison, etc.). If you work in a formal environment where compensation discussions are thorough and highly structured, then walk your boss through the document in real time. But in most cases, a verbal discussion covering the key points will feel more appropriate. Either way, coming prepared will give you confidence and serve as a reference point, if needed. Your plan also offers a tangible asset you can send before or after the conversation, adding weight to your case and leaving a lasting positive impression on your boss.

Settle on a Number

Go in asking for too much and you may come across as naïve or even arrogant. Ask for too little and you may end up settling for a baseline salary you'll have to overcome during the next five to ten years of your career. The national average for a raise across the United States is between 4.5 and 6 percent, but it's not uncommon for me to have clients who have received increases of 10 percent— sometimes 20 percent or more. And if you're following all the steps in this book, then you should ask for more, too. This gives you room to negotiate and meet your employer in the middle, so that both of you feel good about the outcome.

Below are some rules of thumb. Keep in mind: If you have a long tenure and stellar track record at the company, push for the higher end of each range.

- **Ask for 5–10 percent.** If you're more junior or brand-new to the industry, balance ambition and realism. A conservative approach, aiming for a 5–10 percent increase, is often suitable, particularly in fiscally conservative companies or in sectors with traditional raise structures. A smaller raise may be the most reliable option if you're nearing the top of the salary range for your level.

- **Ask for 10–15 percent.** Mid-level professionals with a longer tenure or track record of results may be able to ask for a more substantial increase of 10–15 percent. This is especially true if your pay is already competitive for your job, but you have continued to perform above expectations.

- **Ask for 15–25 percent.** Senior leaders with extensive experience can often justify larger increases because of their direct impact on revenue generation. Requesting a raise of 15–25 percent is bold, but it may be appropriate if you're in high demand in your field, you've taken on significant responsibility without a compensation adjustment, or you're severely underpaid relative to industry standards. This is a *big* jump, so come armed with extremely strong salary market data and clear examples of how your contributions have boosted the bottom line.

Do a gut check and compare your number against market rates. Websites like Glassdoor, Payscale, and Salary.com allow you to enter your job title, location, years of experience, and other relevant factors to get a baseline salary estimate. Just remember, if your responsibilities exceed your current title, you may want to research salaries for the next level up versus your current role. You can also ask HR to give you information about where you fall within the salary band for your level.

Another helpful, albeit nerve-racking, strategy is to ask your close co-workers and colleagues what they make: "I saw on Salary .com that our job pays $X. Does that sound about right to you?," "I'm thinking about asking to bring my salary to a range of $X to $Y. Does that sound fair in your experience?," or "My review is coming up, and I'm making $X. How much would be appropriate to ask for?" You can even blame me and share, "I just read in a book that it can be helpful to get an understanding of what your peers make, both financially and from an equality standpoint. So, if you'd be willing to share what your comp package looks like, I'm happy to do the same. This stays between the two of us. I can go first." I know it can be tricky to ask, but the alternative is to be in the dark and be underpaid, which is never appealing.

Get a Meeting on the Books

Choose a time when your manager is least likely to be stressed or overwhelmed, avoiding busy periods like the end of a quarter, major project deadlines, or industry-wide crunches (like the lead-up to April 15 if you're an accountant). Instead of springing the conversation on your manager unexpectedly, give them a heads-up and time to prepare. Broach the topic in your next one-on-one or send an email with a subject line like "Compensation Discussion" using one or a combination of the following scripts:

- **The direct approach.** "I've been reflecting on the value I bring to the team and would like to explore the possibility of a salary adjustment based on my contributions. Can we set a time to chat about this in the next few weeks?"

- **The achievement-oriented angle.** "I wanted to touch base about the successes we've had recently, particularly [specific project or accomplishment] and how that shows my growing contribution to the team. When would be a good time to talk about how this is reflected in my compensation?"

- **The future-focused script.** "I've been thinking about my career path and future here, which includes considering my compensation. I'd appreciate the opportunity to chat about this with you and get your insights. When would be a good time for us to sit down?"

- **The market rate mention.** "I've been doing some research on market rates for my position and skill set, and I'd like to review my findings with you in relation to my current salary. It's important to me that my compensation aligns with the industry standards. Can we set aside some time to go over this?"

- **The advancement conversation add-on.** "As I continue to take on more responsibilities, I think it's a good time to discuss how my salary reflects these developments and to make

sure my compensation aligns with the evolving scope of
my role. Could we have a conversation about this soon?"

Book twenty to thirty minutes for the actual money conversation, not an hour. This allows enough time to present the document you prepared or talk through the highlights of your business
case without it awkwardly dragging on. If your situation is particularly complex (e.g., you have to negotiate an entirely new contract),
a longer meeting or multiple discussions might be necessary.

Make Your Ask

When the time comes, don't beat around the bush and make small
talk. Start with gratitude and a clearly stated purpose: "I appreciate you taking the time for this meeting. My goal is to have an
open conversation about my salary, particularly in light of [spe-
cific reason]" or "Thanks for your time today. I'd like to focus on
my compensation and explore the possibility of an adjustment
considering [specific reason]." Tee up your business case (e.g., "I'd
like to share some insights on my past contributions and how I
see my role evolving to be an asset here") and walk your boss
through both key quantifiable wins you've achieved as well as
how you plan to expand your impact (e.g., "Looking ahead, I plan
to leverage my expertise in X to enhance Y process, which could
lead to Z benefits"). People are more likely to respond positively to
a request if they perceive it as fair, so next say something like "In
light of what I've just shared, I'd like to talk about an adjustment
to my current compensation" or "It seems appropriate to consider
how my salary reflects these results."

Since asking for money is one of—if not the most—complex,

high-tension issues you'll face in your professional life, it's better to have more ways to talk about it than fewer. Customize these additional scripts according to what you've learned about your manager's communication style and personality throughout this book, especially from chapters 1 and 2:

- Given my accomplishments over the last X months, I'd like to revisit my salary and make sure it matches with industry standards.

- I've done my research and found that my salary is below average for my position and location. I'm hoping we can work together to find a reasonable solution.

- Based on my recent achievements, including [result], I'm thinking an increase along the lines of [percentage or amount] would be warranted.

- I've taken on more responsibility this year and have had significant successes, like [result]. I feel a [percentage or amount] increase in my salary would reflect the value I've added.

- Based on my research, I'd like to propose a salary adjustment to [amount], which I feel matches my contributions and market rates.

- As we plan for [upcoming project or period], and given my role in [specific area], an increase to [amount] would reflect how my role has evolved.

- I've been pivotal in [achievement or project], and I believe it's fair for this to be reflected in my compensation. I'd like to propose a salary increase to [amount].

- After looking at the scope of my current role, my
  performance, and industry benchmarks, I believe a raise
  to [amount] would be fair.

Deliver your number and *stop talking*. Silence is power. Negotiators who pause are seen as more confident, capable, and credible.
Silence also creates tension, which leads others to make concessions in order to end the discomfort.

Respond to Resistance

No matter how hard you work, what you've accomplished, and how
well you present your case, your manager may be hesitant to give you
more money for reasons that are beyond your control. If it's early in
your career or you're new in your role, you'll need to be careful about
pushing too hard since you have less power. The more senior or ten-
ured you are, the more leverage you probably have to position yourself as a partner to your boss and have a collaborative dialogue that
reflects your experience and contributions within the organization.

- **If they blame budget constraints, try:** "Can you share more?
  That might help us find a middle ground that works for
  both of us" or "I understand. Maybe we could explore
  performance-based incentives or a deferred raise that
  goes into effect when finances improve?"

- **If they cite company rules or timing, try:** "Are there
  precedents or exceptions where these policies have been
  adjusted?" or "Since my next review is [time frame], can
  we use that opportunity to discuss an increase?"

- **If they want more evidence of your results, try:** "What outcomes or milestones would you need to see from me to feel comfortable granting a raise?" or "I'll continue documenting my achievements and impact with the understanding that we'll reassess again in X months. Does that work?"

- **If they say giving you more money wouldn't be fair to others, try:** "How do we differentiate roles based on contribution levels, and could my raise reflect this differentiation?" or "Could we explore how raises are determined across the team to ensure we're rewarding individual performance fairly?"

- **If they say business is too uncertain, try:** "What are the specific challenges we're facing? I'd like to make sure my efforts are addressing these issues" or "If a salary increase is off the table for now, could we consider other benefits like stock options or professional development opportunities?" (We'll touch on other nonmonetary benefits you can ask for in a moment!)

It can be frustrating and demoralizing to hear anything other than an enthusiastic yes accompanied by a meaningful increase. Whatever your boss says or suggests, don't feel the need to respond immediately. Ask for a day or two to consider their offer and let the heat of the moment pass so you can accept gracefully or present a thoughtful counter-proposal.

When Neha was considered for her boss's role, she had hoped for $100,000, toward the higher end of market salaries for the role, but received an offer of only $85,000. She then formulated options, each of which would meet many of her most important interests. First, if not $100,000, she'd accept $95,000 with her current benefits, especially if the pay could be revisited at the six month mark. She would also consider $90,000 if they could give her an extra week of vacation. Finally, if $85,000 was truly the best they could do, then she'd need two additional weeks of vacation and flexible working hours to compensate. Having this layered set of options gave Neha peace of mind that she wouldn't freeze or nervously accept a less than favorable arrangement.

Notice how her options included nonmonetary compensation, which can be just as valuable and sometimes easier for decision-makers to agree to. Consider concessions your company may be more amenable to than cash. If you're more seasoned, you have more sway to ask for a title change, a better office, equity, or even a stipend to redo your home office. Junior and mid-level employees may have better luck getting benefits like flexible work hours, remote workdays, professional-development or transportation reimbursements, and extra vacation days. You could even negotiate to lead new projects, to attend certain meetings or planning sessions that are typically reserved for higher-level staff, or to adjust your job responsibilities to align more with your strengths.

Despite all your preparation and best efforts to implement everything in this chapter, you may hear no or "let's table this." Politely ask for the rejection to be documented: "Would it be possible to get this in writing, along with the rationale? It would help me understand and plan my next steps accordingly." Having to justify the decision formally can sometimes lead them to a reassessment, and at the very least gives you a paper trail. Ask for a future endorsement with phrases like "If I continue to meet and exceed our key metrics, could I count on your support for a salary review in the next fiscal year?" or "I understand there are constraints right now. Would you be willing to support a raise in the future, provided I continue to deliver?"

Beyond the Conversation

Work Your *Ask* Off

Whether it's the fear that your request will be denied, worry over how you'll be perceived, or anxiety about justifying your number, the money conversation can come with a lot of intense emotions. But the more you confront your discomfort head-on, the less fearful you become. Your brain will gradually start to recognize that there's no need to freak out when the topic of finances comes up (called habituation) because you can handle it. Over the next week or two, find low-pressure settings in which to talk about money. Maybe you negotiate your phone or internet bill, haggle at a flea market, or set up a once-monthly meeting with your partner to review expenses. The more you practice, the easier and more natural talking about money will feel—and the more confident you'll become.

Another way to get exposure is to advocate on behalf of others, whether it's better equipment for your team, more budget for initiatives, or securing raises or bonuses to reward your employees. As always, align your request with your boss's goals and priorities. For example, if your boss is focused on conserving the budget, "We need more staff to handle our workload" could be switched to "We could hire two junior stylists at lower starting salaries and then upskill them over time, which would be a smarter long-term investment." Make it clear that you're not here to deceive or exploit your boss or the company by using phrases like "I'm willing to be flexible" or

"I'm happy to consider other options," which show that you're open to compromise and willing to adjust your position if necessary.

Pitch Even from a Distance

Virtual work is here to stay, which means you'll often be having the money conversation digitally. This doesn't necessarily put you at a disadvantage, but it does require you to pay more attention to nuances of your body language. Research by Vanessa Van Edwards, author of *Cues* and lead investigator at Science of People, has found that the brain gives 12.5 times more weight to hand gestures and that simply tilting your palms up at a forty-five-degree angle signals candor and openness, as if to say, "See, I have nothing to hide!"

Not only does this create transparency, breaking the tension during a salary discussion, but studies also find that hand gestures help you remember what you're going to say. But Van Edwards advises you to "stay in the box": "Appropriate hand-speaking space is from the top of your chest to the bottom of your waist. If you go outside this box, it's seen as distracting and out of control." Sit an arm's length away from your screen so you have enough room to move around.

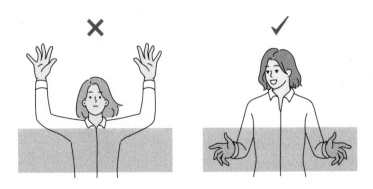

Stay away from "self-touching gestures," like fiddling with your hair or jewelry, pulling at your collar, or rubbing your forehead—all of which can make you appear unprepared or insecure. And here's another key tip: Turn off the self-view option on your video software if possible. The "constant mirror" effect of staring at yourself on video is distracting, draining, and likely to increase feelings of self-consciousness.

What to Do When . . .

You Face Bias

Pay discrimination takes many forms, from statements like "Aren't you already getting paid enough?" to your boss giving your peer's team double the resources despite the fact that they have half the experience. Whether you're the one affected or you want to be an ally to someone else, here are initial steps to take:

- **Change from "I" to "it."** I learned this trick from Kim Scott, author of *Radical Candor*. Instead of "*I* don't think that I'm paid enough," say "*It* doesn't seem right that the same work is being paid at different rates." Instead of "*I* think you pay the men who work here more," try "*It* looks like male colleagues have higher salaries." Shifting focus to the *behavior* that needs to be addressed can be more powerful and convincing.

- **Make the invisible visible.** Request transparency around pay processes and criteria for determining where money goes: "Where can I find details about how compensation is calculated?" or "How do we determine which initiatives get funded?"

- **Call them in (or out).** One portfolio manager, an Asian woman, told me, "I managed to get my direct report equal pay to her male counterpart after I mentioned that asking her to take on more work without additional pay would be an example of us contributing to the gender pay gap." You might even suggest a team- or company-wide compensation audit for fairness and competitiveness: "After gathering input from different team members, we've noticed a pattern of pay discrepancies. I've known other companies to hire an external agency to make sure compensation is fair. Is that something we'd consider?"

- **Go on the record.** Document any conversations that show discriminatory behavior and screenshot digital conversations (text, email, or work chat). Voice your concerns to HR in writing so that there's evidence both you and the company know about your manager's actions. You can also request that a neutral third party—such as an HR rep or another supervisor— join any high-stakes money conversations going forward.

- **Know your rights.** Advocate for everyone by sharing articles, talking to colleagues, and participating in events regarding pay equity. Familiarize yourself with the U.S. Equal Employment Opportunity Commission (EEOC) laws as well as legal guidelines in your state and any specific company policies that could be relevant. Find out if your company has an anonymous reporting line, an employee resource group, or other diversity and inclusion resources that can support you.

You Have Another Offer

Maybe you've been interviewing just to see what's out there and to keep your skills sharp. Maybe a job opportunity came to you. Whatever the case, you're now faced with an offer from another company. The pay is enticing, but you'd love to stay at your current job—albeit with a better paycheck. How do you leverage an external offer delicately without it being perceived by your boss as a threat or sign of disloyalty?

- **Weigh the risks.** Yes, studies show that when people ask for a raise with an outside offer in hand, their request is perceived as more legitimate and justified. But this can easily strain your relationships. Your boss and other higher-ups may not only feel blindsided but also worry about your commitment to the company. Only bring up an external offer if one or more factors are true: You're truly happy to accept a counteroffer to stay at your current company, you have very strong rapport with your manager, you aren't worried about retaliation, and you work in an industry like higher education, engineering, or consulting, where this is standard practice.

- **Ask for a match.** If you do decide to bring your external offer to the negotiating table, emphasize your loyalty and desire to stay in your current role: "I've received an offer

from another company that's 20 percent higher than my
current salary. I genuinely enjoy working here and my
intention isn't to leave, so I wanted to see if [current
company] could match the compensation." Keep your
tone positive to show that you're reasonable, yet
understand your value.

- **Consider their counteroffer.** Analyze not just the salary but
  also any changes in benefits, responsibilities, or job title
  that come with it. How does it compare to the external
  offer? If the counteroffer is below your expectations but
  still within a range you consider acceptable, try more
  negotiating: "I'm excited about continuing to grow with
  the company. I'm prepared to stay on board if we can
  adjust the bonus structure to bring my total
  compensation in line with market rates."

- **Be prepared to walk.** Your boss may balk in the moment
  (e.g., "So why don't you take the other offer then?") or
  you may find out they're unable to get a match approved.
  If that happens, be ready to accept the external offer;
  otherwise, your attempt to negotiate will seem like mere
  bluffing. Knowing that you backed down from your
  position could lead to less leverage in all your future
  interactions, not just about money. Plus, choosing to stay
  can create a perception that you're just biding your time
  before something better comes along, leading you to be
  sidelined because you're seen as having one foot out the
  door.

- **Don't overplay your hand.** Leveraging an external offer may
  work once—and possibly twice—in any organization,
  but not more than that. Management likely won't

continue to reward someone who pulls this move every year. So use this tactic sparingly and only when significant discrepancies in compensation arise.

You've been patient and understanding in the face of resistance to your requests for a salary increase. You've continued to do your best work and spearheaded new initiatives without a change in pay. Maybe you've even turned down offers from other companies because you're sure senior management will come through, only to find that at the end of the quarter or at the end of the year, they don't . . . again. If you've repeatedly had the money conversation (or any of the conversations in this book) to no avail, it's likely time to consider moving on. Sometimes the only way to jump to a different salary band is to switch companies. In the next chapter, we'll talk about how to have the quitting conversation.

CHAPTER TEN

The Quitting Conversation

Say goodbye without burning bridges

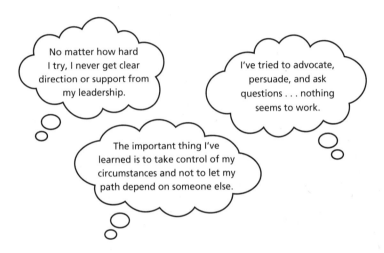

Remember when I shared my story of being laid off in chapter 1? Even though it took several years to reclaim my sense of confidence, I don't regret that it happened. In addition to propelling my coaching business forward, it also forced me to rethink the way I operated at work. Those insights have paid enormous dividends for me and my clients, and in the years since, I've had the opportunity to see things come full circle. I now have former colleagues from that healthcare company (let's call it Acme Corp) seek me out for guidance regarding their own careers.

Take Jade, a director who joined one of my programs after Acme was acquired by a bigger insurance company. During the past decade, Jade had grown and evolved her role multiple times from research manager to head of clinical education to project management within their growing IT infrastructure to business analytics.

Jade now reported to Alexi, a leader from the insurance side she respected (and who respected her!). After a few months of feeling out the new landscape, Jade felt ready to have the advancement conversation. "I was eager to make better use of my brain," she told me. "Business analysis was fun for a while, but dealing in operations and our tech stack felt stale." She went to Alexi with a plan. What if she parlayed her experience into an innovation role? She pitched him on the idea of researching trends in patient care and developing new ideas that would reduce costs and add new revenue streams.

"That's interesting," he said, "but I don't think there's an appetite for it."

Jade was frustrated. She had always been a trailblazer at Acme who charted her own course, but now she felt hemmed in. She vowed to remain patient, telling herself that Alexi's response wasn't personal. After all, the merger was brand-new, and things were sure to get better. During the next six months, Jade tried other ways to take ownership, thinking she could earn trust and credibility from her new colleagues that would eventually allow her to utilize the creativity and agility that had made her so successful up until now. "At every turn I was told by the powers that be 'not yet.' I couldn't believe that I was asking to *work more* and they said no!"

After a year without any progress or change, Alexi pulled her aside after a meeting during which she had offered to take on a new project and was shot down. "I don't want to lose you," he confessed, "but you need to leave. You deserve to be somewhere where your talents are valued, and you don't meet so much resistance."

The thought of walking away filled Jade with sadness and dread, especially because she had never had to confront the awkwardness of giving notice. But as she weighed her options, she found that daydreaming about her next chapter filled her with excitement and anticipation. The time had come to have *the quitting conversation* so that she could leave on good terms with her relationships and respect intact.

Departing in a blaze of glory and giving your former boss and colleagues the middle finger can sound appealing, but just as you never get a second chance to make a first impression, the same can be said for making a last impression. Thanks to the peak-end effect, people's memories are heavily influenced by how an experience ends, so how you exit a role is often just as important as how you perform in it when it comes to the kind of reference you'll get from the company or manager. Will others remember you as someone who made everyone's life easier by communicating a transition plan clearly, continued to pitch in on projects, and thanked others as you walked out the door? Or will they think of you as someone who slowly faded away and lost focus once you turned in your notice?

You might be thinking, "But I know I'm leaving. Who cares about managing up at this point?" The reality is that most quitting conversations are less of a "goodbye" and more of a "see you later." More than 70 percent of professionals have landed a job at some point in their careers through their network, which often includes former leaders and colleagues. Whether it's seeking a reference, proposing a collaboration, or needing a favor from someone in your old company, the way you manage your exit could very well determine people's willingness to vouch for you or open doors in the future. Some industries, such as tech and finance, are known for having a "small world" effect. Your ex-boss from a startup could end up as a senior executive in a major company you later aspire to join. A former colleague from your investment banking days might reappear as a client, a competitor, or even a regulator. Plus, you never know when or if you'll want to be rehired by the same company. Nearly 30 percent of employees "boomerang," returning to their old role within thirteen months of quitting.

Regardless of the situation—be it a harmonious departure or one under challenging conditions—you'll know you acted in a way you feel proud of. And that's exactly what this chapter will help you do.

Should You Stay or Should You Go?

The best career decisions balance head and heart. In fact, pairing intuition with analytical thinking helps you make better, faster, and more accurate decisions and gives you more confidence in your choices than relying on intellect alone, especially when there's no "correct" option. For instance, if you're torn between staying in a stable job or jumping into a new opportunity that seems risky, your instinct about what will bring you the most long-term happiness can guide you. Choosing between two job offers with similar salaries but very different cultures might come down to a gut feeling about where you'd fit best. So use one or more of the following exercises to make sure you're leaving for reasons you feel good about.

Role-Play It

Reggie had worked at a public policy think tank for three years when he received a research director offer from a corporate public relations firm that regularly used his studies in their project work. On paper, both paths (staying and leaving) offered positives and negatives, so I gave him an experiment. For three days, he was to act as if he had chosen to stay in his current role and observe his reactions. What was he thinking? How did he feel? Then, for another three days, he was to "try on" the idea of leaving and pursuing the consulting path.

After a week, Reggie's choice was clear. When he considered staying, he felt heavy, as if he were walking around with a cloud over his head. When he thought about leaving, his mind buzzed with ideas, and he approached conversations with energy and vigor. Simulating the outcome can tell you a lot about what you really want. You can also try flipping a coin and seeing how you feel about the answer. If heads means quitting, do you feel joy and relief? Or worry and resistance?

Flash Forward to Your Future Self

Imagine that you're ninety years old and looking back at this moment in time. What decision would make you feel proud? When faced with a tough or scary career decision, picture yourself old and gray, telling your grandchildren about your life. In that reflection, if you take the path you're considering, will you be more likely to regret that path or regret *not* having taken it?

If it's too difficult to imagine your future self, consider what your personal hero might do. Bring to mind someone you respect, like a colleague, public figure, mentor, or family member.

What would they do if they were in your shoes? Thinking about the people in your life who inspire you can provide fresh insight that guides your decision. It can also get you out of your head, giving you just enough distance to see your choice more objectively.

Walk Through the Worst-Case Scenario

For each option, imagine how you'd handle your nightmare scenario. Take the example of moving across the country for a job. Maybe the worst that could happen is that you despise the cold weather, you feel harried because every daycare has a six-month waiting list, and you're heartbroken seeing your spouse moping around feeling isolated. How would you deal? I bet you'd come up with a plan, whether taking an extra trip somewhere warm, creating a regular routine of virtual family meet-ups, or joining a parenting group for camaraderie and nanny sharing.

After that, go to the other extreme and contemplate the upside. What if you loved the change of pace from a small town to a big city? What if your spouse and kids found fulfilling hobbies of their own? Confronting your fears (known as defensive pessimism in psychology) helps you feel more in control and capable of handling challenges, while channeling your optimistic side can help you feel more comfortable with your choice.

Bidding Adieu, Without Saying "Screw You"

You've made the decision: It's time to go! What's the best way to gracefully quit while still maintaining your relationships? How do you avoid burning bridges?

Play Defense

Even if you've worked for the company for a long time and generally have a good relationship with your boss, you may be told to pack up your things then and there. So before doing anything else, back up any documents, projects, and contact information that belongs to you but lives on your work computer or phone. Avoid taking proprietary or sensitive company information to steer clear of legal issues.

Assuming you've been documenting your achievements as we've talked about in prior chapters, refresh your metrics and portfolio while you still have access to precise sales numbers, analytics reports, or budget sheets. For digital work like website designs or social media campaigns, take screenshots and annotate explanations of what they show and your role in these projects while it's fresh in your mind. Thank me later when you're not grasping for impressive details to fill out your résumé and LinkedIn profile! Save copies of your past performance reviews, too.

Whatever you do, don't spill the beans to your co-workers before telling your boss. It's tempting to let your work besties in on your plans, but if the information leaks, it'll leave a bad taste in everyone's mouth (e.g., "Why did so-and-so know before I did?"). It might even be interpreted as a lack of professional courtesy or respect, potentially leading to you being let go prematurely. By informing your boss first (which we'll focus on in the next step), you maintain greater control over the timeline and narrative of your departure. Staying employed until your planned resignation date also means you continue to receive your salary and benefits (like health insurance) for that period, which is important if you don't have another job lined up. Besides, an amicable parting—rather than a forced exit—is a lot easier to explain in future interviews.

Break the News

Now comes the hard part. Set up a one-on-one meeting with your boss outside of your regularly scheduled meetings to deliver your resignation. Face-to-face is ideal, but virtual works, too. Breaking the news via phone or email can seem cold and cowardly. For example, you might say, "Do you have some time to meet on [day]? I have something important to discuss, and I think it would be best to talk about it in person."

Your manager might suspect that something is up from the outset, so get straight to the point: "I've decided it's time for me to move on. My last day will be March 24" or "This isn't an easy decision, but I am resigning from my role as head of consumer goods effective immediately." Rehearse what you'll say in advance, along with a response to "But why are you leaving?" Even if you're getting out because of a toxic environment, now is not the time for the feedback conversation. What you say could be mentioned to prospective employers, and negativity isn't going to get you a positive recommendation. Keep your responses forward-looking and focused on your own growth and development. Don't apologize, overexplain, or gush about the details and perks of your new venture. Here's a few ways to deliver the news:

- It's been an honor to work with such a dedicated and talented team, and I'm ready for a new challenge.

- I've appreciated the opportunities I've had here, but I've decided to pursue a role that aligns with my strengths and interests a bit more.

- Lately, I've been drawn to [new field/industry]. I've been offered a job in this area that I can't pass up, so I feel it's the right time for me to make this transition.

- I'm grateful for all my experiences and learnings here. Next, I'll be taking time off to spend with my family and take care of my health.

- I've thought more about the kind of work environment and culture that I thrive in, and I've realized that I want to explore a different setting. This is about my personal preference and where I see myself fitting best.

Your manager might be shocked, especially if they didn't see it coming; sad or disappointed because they really value your work; or frustrated that you're leaving in the middle of a busy time or important projects. Stay calm, reaffirm your decision, and redirect the conversation to next steps: "I recognize this timing might not be ideal, and I'm here to do whatever it takes to minimize any disruption" or "I can understand that this is hard news and took you by surprise. I've considered this carefully and know it's time for me to take on a new challenge. So I hope we can focus on how to make this change as positive as possible."

STEAL THIS SCRIPT

Right after you've spoken with your manager, use the template below to email your letter of resignation and put your notice in writing.

SUBJECT: [Your name]'s Resignation Letter
Dear [Manager name],

Thank you for speaking with me today. I've appreciated these past [number of] years at [company]. I wanted to inform you that my last day of work at [company] will be on [date].

During my time here, I've gained valuable skills, experience, and connections. I'm grateful for the opportunity to hone my [skill set], grow as a/an [job title] professional, and contribute to the company.

Before I leave, I'll ensure that all my projects are completed as much as possible. As I mentioned when we spoke, I'm happy to assist in the handover to my replacement.

All the best,
[Your signature]

Contend with a Counteroffer

Your manager or others may dangle more money and perks in front of you to get you to stay. A counteroffer could be made the moment you break the news or one may come a few days or a week later once your manager consults with HR and upper management. Don't bet on it being a game changer.

Even if there's nothing that could get you to stay, take a beat and bide your time rather than responding on the spot: "I need some time to mull over what you've offered and to consider my options. Can I get back to you in a few days with my final decision?" This is about optics—showing respect to your boss and the organization, acknowledging the effort they made to keep you, and giving the impression that you're a thoughtful, thorough professional who weighs things carefully.

If, after contemplation, you decide you're still ready to go, reiter-ate your stance: "Thank you for the gesture to change my title, but my mind is made up" or "I'm flattered by the counteroffer, but my decision to leave is final." If your boss becomes irate or defensive (e.g., "Do you know what I had to go through to get this deal for you?"), try to smooth things over: "I understand and I respect your feelings, but I believe this is the best decision for me right now. I know my exit will be an adjustment for the team, so I'm happy to train my replacement and have prepared a transition plan so the business doesn't miss a beat after my last day."

In the event the company comes back with something extremely appealing (rare, but it happens), or you want to say yes to buy yourself a couple months of paid work while lining up another job, you can also counter with something like "The salary adjustment does address one of my main concerns. I was also hoping for more career develop-ment opportunities and greater flexibility for work-life balance. If we could find a way to address these areas as well, it would create a com-pelling reason for me to reconsider my decision." If you do decide to accept, agree on timelines for when changes will go into effect. Get the terms in writing so that you understand any expectations or con-ditions that come with it. Keep a record of all emails, memos, and meeting notes so you have documentation should misunderstandings arise or if you need to escalate the matter.

Transition Out Tactfully

While giving at least two weeks' notice is standard practice in the United States and most countries, you may give more or less notice depending on the situation, your tenure, and your local laws. I never recommend giving more than two to three months' notice because it gets messy for everyone. Consider what happened to

Michelle, a caseworker at a city child welfare agency. In the beginning of January, Michelle told her boss she'd be leaving to pursue private practice and wanted to have all her work wrapped up by the end of June. Michelle's boss, grateful for the heads-up, began assigning other team members parts of Michelle's client load within a few weeks. But the premature handoff created confusion. The new caseworkers were unsure about whether to approach Michelle or her boss for guidance, which led to duplicate effort. As she was gradually left out of key meetings and critical communications, Michelle felt marginalized and caught in an uncomfortable limbo. The buildup of tension led Michelle's boss to terminate her contract before the end of May, much earlier than her planned departure.

If you move on without properly handing off your role, you risk leaving a legacy of disarray. Creating a transition plan shows that you're thinking not just about your own future but also about the continuity and well-being of the team and projects you're leaving behind. Your colleagues may not be thrilled to pick up your slack, but they'll respect the fact that you've tried to make their jobs easier.

At a bare minimum, list all your daily tasks, weekly responsibilities, and any other duties you perform regularly. Don't overlook tasks that might seem routine but are crucial to operations (monitoring office supplies, regular software backups, processing invoices, etc.). For bigger, more complex projects, note their stage—initial planning, in progress, or near completion—as well as any upcoming deadlines or key milestones. If you have the time and inclination, write down or screen record detailed instructions on how to perform each task or responsibility.

Knowledge transfer is crucial, too. Share a list of internal and external contacts—stakeholders, clients, vendors, and team members.

Safely compile and pass along necessary logins for systems, tools, or resources you manage. You might even think about potential questions or challenges your successor might face and provide answers or solutions in a FAQ section. Include insider tips you've learned that make the process more efficient or client preferences, for instance.

Beyond the Conversation

Craft Your Comms Strategy

After you've discussed your resignation with your manager, figure out who needs to know what and by when, being sure to coordinate with any HR announcements or procedural requirements as well. When Tina, a motion graphic designer on Kyle's team, told him midway through film production that she was leaving, he was determined to avoid an acute case of quitting contagion infecting the crew. He and Tina crafted a message that made it clear Tina was taking a role as a visual effects supervisor, a big step up from her current position, rather than allowing people to draw their own conclusions about internal conflict or turmoil. First, Kyle called his boss, and he and Tina met with her that afternoon. From there, they decided how, when, and in what order they would notify different stakeholders. They started with those on a "need to know basis," including having Tina meet with each of her direct reports and sending a mass email to those in the adjacent art departments that would be most impacted. Throughout her last two weeks, she was grateful that she and Kyle had crafted talking points she could refer to again and again. She even took time to recommend one of her colleagues for her position, which Kyle appreciated.

Close colleagues and direct team members should usually be first to know (as in the example with Kyle and Tina), followed by contacts in other departments and business units. In general, it's standard practice to inform internal stakeholders before notifying external clients or partners about your resignation to ensure a unified message gets out. That said, if you've developed a particularly close professional relationship with a client, for example, and your departure will directly affect their ongoing projects or contract, it may be appropriate to inform them shortly after your manager and immediate team are aware, especially if they are due to make critical business decisions based on your involvement.

Redirect or Say No to New Requests

Once you have the quitting conversation, you don't have to pretend to be all in anymore, but you shouldn't entirely check out either. Even in your final days, colleagues may still come to you with new work. When they do, don't jump to complete the task simply to get it off your plate. Instead, offer to train them on how to complete it for themselves or coach them through how to perform a process as you learned to do as part of the feedback conversation in chapter 5. Not only does this set a boundary, but it empowers your colleagues to take ownership and become more self-sufficient, which they'll need to do in your absence. There may be cases where you have to say no to a request altogether:

- That's not something I'm able to take on with my last day approaching.

- I have to decline, since I won't be here to see this through.

- Thanks for thinking of me. At the same time, I'll have to pass in order to get my current projects done.

Be careful not to make an open-ended invitation to consult or provide assistance beyond your final day at the company. Answering a question here and there is understandable. Pick a date (perhaps two to four weeks after your departure) by which you'll no longer be available. If the questions continue past that time, you may have to send a final note explaining you won't be responding in order to focus on your current role and wish them all the best.

What to Do When . . .

You're Asked to Do an Exit Interview

The exit interview is a standard part of most employee offboarding processes, and it's designed to benefit your employer, giving them information that could help them address employee turnover or broader inefficiencies. Speaking your mind freely—and knowing your feedback could spark constructive change—can feel satisfying, too. It's possible that what you share could influence a job reference check in the future, though, so choose your words wisely. Here's how to approach the process from a strategic perspective:

- **Think carefully before agreeing.** It's okay to decline an exit interview, especially if you're not in a good mental space to participate—if you're feeling highly emotional or even generally stressed about the transition process. Before deciding, ask HR or your manager how the information you share will be used, who will have access to it, and how the company intends to act on the input. Look for assurances that your feedback will be anonymized or kept confidential to prevent retaliation. The company should explain how they share findings with leadership and develop action plans for improvement. Ask for examples of past changes made based on exit interview feedback.

- **Gather your thoughts.** HR typically conducts these sessions, but in some circumstances, your or another team's manager will join. Be prepared to answer questions like: What led you to look for another position? What helped you do your job well, and what hindered it? What recommendations do you have for onboarding new employees? How do you feel about your former colleagues and managers? What were the best and worst parts of working in this position?

- **Write your rant down.** Do a brain dump of all your grievances to process your anger, resentment, and frustration. Let your responses sit overnight. Once you've allowed your initial emotions to settle, revisit your notes with a clear head and outline three to four bullet points of diplomatic ways to respond to the questions above. For each point of criticism, try to suggest a potential solution or recommendation that could help the company improve.

- **Keep things positive.** In the actual exit interview, begin each response on a positive note about your experience, then gently segue into your suggestions: "Everyone was welcoming, and I think more structured onboarding

could help all newcomers get up to speed faster" or "I
learned a lot by working with clients, but I would have
liked training on dealing with contract disputes. I
struggled with that and didn't get the support I was
hoping for from my manager."

- **Be bland.** If you don't feel comfortable or safe sharing
  feedback, be vague in your responses, but keep a friendly,
  professional tone to avoid appearing disinterested or
  dismissive. Why are you leaving? *I found a great
  opportunity elsewhere that fits my career goals.* Would you
  recommend others work here? *It's a great fit for someone
  looking for a challenging and dynamic environment.*

You're Leaving on Not-So-Great Terms

Even if you've made every effort to be gracious and helpful during
your exit, it's possible that your boss might still feel resentful or
upset about your exit. Immature? Maybe, but it happens. You can't
control their reaction, but you can do the following to leave with
your head held high:

- **Express just enough gratitude.** A goodbye email one or two
  days in advance of your last day can be a small way to
  mend things with your manager, but don't overdo it. If
  your relationship is or was rocky, avoid effusive, overly
  emotional language and high praise that can seem
  insincere (e.g., "I can't express how much I've enjoyed
  working with you. I'll cherish the experience forever").
  Stick to something more believable and less intense like:

"Thank you for your leadership at [company]. Working on [specific project] has been particularly valuable for my professional growth. I've gained a lot of skills here that I'll take with me into my next role."

- **Identify other references.** Whether you're leaving without another job lined up and plan to be interviewing, or you've already secured a new position, you want to make sure that when you leave your current role there are people at the company who will vouch for you in the future. If your relationship with your boss is strained, they may not provide the most favorable reference. So identify other colleagues, leaders, supervisors, or clients who can speak positively about your work and character and explicitly ask for their endorsement: "As I'm transitioning to [this new opportunity / the next phase of my career], would you be comfortable if I listed you as a reference?"

- **Shape the narrative.** Your boss might intentionally or unintentionally share a skewed version of how and why you left the company with colleagues or industry contacts, which could impact your reputation. Frame your transition as a step forward rather than a contentious exit by posting to social media, mentioning the valuable experiences you gained and the skills you developed in your last role and your enthusiasm for your next opportunity. Likewise, leave LinkedIn recommendations for colleagues with whom you had a good working relationship to build goodwill and act as a public testament to your collegiality and professionalism.

- **Create closure.** All humans have a natural desire for cognitive closure, which is why it can feel so unsettling not getting an apology or a chance to clear the air with your manager. Create a sense of finality for yourself. Perhaps you archive your work files, throw out company swag, or shred unnecessary documents. These rituals provide a tangible sense of completion, helping you to mentally move forward with confidence and peace.

- **Explain what happened without bashing your old boss.** In interviews, instead of saying, "I had some problems with my manager" or "I didn't like the company culture," frame your departure as a proactive step rather than an escape from a bad situation: "After four years in my last role, I'm ready for a new environment," "I valued my time at [old organization], but felt it was time to expand my skill set," or "As I've refined my expertise in [area], I've realized that [new company] offers the most opportunity to grow."

The ten conversations aren't one-time talks. As you move through different phases and encounter changes—starting a new job, adjusting to a reorg, joining a new workgroup—you'll find yourself revisiting the conversations in this book again and again. Switched bosses? Time to revisit the alignment and styles conversations so you can quickly adapt and hit the ground running. Bagged a promotion? The visibility conversation may take on new significance as you try to get attention from more senior stakeholders. At every stage, you're building on a foundation you've already set, becoming more in tune with the subtleties of your workplace relationships, and more capable of steering your career in the direction you want it to go. It's an ongoing process, one where the learning never really stops, and honestly, that's the exciting part.

Turn Your Insight into Action

You deserve better than just "getting by" at work. You deserve to feel like you're in the driver's seat of your career and to feel confident, valued, and strong when interacting with those above you. Managing up may not feel natural at first, especially if you've spent a long time working for a boss who seems to be speaking a different language, or who connects more strongly with certain colleagues of yours, leaving you frustrated and wondering what you're doing wrong. When you've internalized the idea that you're a passenger in your own career, it takes time to build a sense of agency. But now you have the tools to get what you need from the people in charge.

Start small, if you need to—practice asking a probing question in your next one-on-one or share a win with a colleague you look up to. Keep pushing yourself to have the conversations that matter, to take risks and try new things, to advocate for yourself and others with courage and conviction.

Over the years, I've met countless brilliant, creative, and strategic professionals across industries and levels who, despite their talents, have unwittingly been held back because they don't know how to influence without authority. Some mistakenly overstepped unspoken chains of command and proposed ideas at the wrong time or to the wrong people, while others rambled in front of executives instead of making a sharp, impactful point. Then there are those who let little frustrations toward their boss fester until they turn into massive problems or who burn out because they never say no. And let's not forget the many times someone has approached me feeling defeated after being rejected for a raise because they couldn't make a compelling case for more money. It doesn't matter how smart or experienced you are. Without a grasp of the subtle art of managing up, you'll find yourself wrestling with unnecessary stress, feeling stifled, angry, and maybe even full of self-doubt.

Everything you've picked up from this book will allow you to handle the tricky dynamics of your workplace with grace and assurance—none of which requires a dramatic overhaul or changing who you are. As you've discovered, little tweaks can have an outsize impact. Something as simple as seeding your interest early on can mean the difference between facing resistance and getting a well-deserved promotion. Offering gentle course corrections after giving your boss feedback could be exactly what helps a new behavior stick—and lessens your daily frustrations. Inserting social proof can turn you from an unknown quantity into someone who is trusted by senior management.

As you move forward with managing up, remember that there will be successes, and there will undoubtedly be setbacks—both are valuable learning experiences. Stay the course and the conversations will get a bit easier, a bit more natural. Over time, not only will you become better at managing up, but you'll also clarify your own values, goals, and strengths along the way. Keep referring back to this book, keep refining your approach, and keep growing your skills. And don't forget that you can download takeaways from each chapter and templates from the book at my website, managingup.com/bonuses.

As we wrap up, I hope you see that the goal of this book isn't simply to change how you deal with your boss or people in power, but to change how you see *yourself*. Instead of being at the mercy of others' decisions or moods, you now have what you need to take the reins of your professional interactions. You can teach people how to treat you and seize greater control over your work life than you ever thought possible. The emotional intelligence, resilience, and assertiveness you'll build are lifelong assets that will continue to serve you, no matter where your career takes you.

Just as I created the ten conversations as a way for *you* to reclaim a sense of control in your professional life, I know you'll share what you've learned with *others*. Imagine you're chatting with a junior team member who's feeling bored. Instead of simply offering a sympathetic ear, you could guide them through the ownership conversation. Or let's say a friend confesses to you that they're sick of their boss changing priorities every week. That's your cue to share insights from the alignment conversation. By passing on what you've learned, you're doing your part to contribute to workplaces where everyone feels heard and respected and where it's normal to speak up and advocate for what you need.

Consider me a partner in your professional journey from here on. Find me at my website, melodywilding.com, and share with me what you do with your insights. Thank you for allowing me to be your guide, and here's to your success!

ACKNOWLEDGMENTS

First, I have to thank you, my reader, for investing your time and energy in this book. I hope you find the ideas and strategies within these pages both useful and inspiring.

To Leah Trouwborst, my editor at Crown Currency, who believed in the vision for this book from day one. Your wise insight shaped my musings into the book it is today. I can't thank you enough for your fantastic direction, enthusiasm, and partnership. I'd also like to thank Paul Whitlatch, Gillian Blake, Cierra Hinckson, Amy Li, and the entire Crown Currency publishing team for their hard work and support in bringing this book to life.

Lisa DiMona—thank you for once again helping me navigate the ins and outs of the publishing process. Your expertise and steadfast support make every step smoother and less daunting. I'm fortunate to have you in my corner.

I'm indebted to Julie Mosow, my developmental editor and writing partner in crime. I'll say it once and I'll say it again: I couldn't have done this without you. I'll miss our marathon Zoom sessions where we hashed out chapter structures, concepts, and edits, but I'm even more grateful that through this process, I've gained a dear friend.

To my husband, Brian—you are truly the most special person I could ever hope to share my life with. Thank you for being a thought partner, my earliest reader, and switching roles between therapist and cheerleader depending on what I needed most. You held down the fort and gave me the space and unconditional support necessary to make this book a reality. I love you with my whole heart.

I'm grateful to my family for their unwavering encouragement and belief not only through the journey of writing this book but in all aspects of my career. Mom and Dad, thank you for being my biggest fans. Your faith in my abilities drives me to reach higher. To my in-laws, Dianne and Barry, thank you for always being there to help Brian and me sort through any issue. Your generosity and love mean the world.

Thank you to my friends who reached out to check in, asked about the book, and offered kind words along the way. Every seemingly small gesture kept me motivated and lifted my spirits during challenging moments.

To my small but mighty team—Rebekah Rius, Sarah Doige, and Riley Limbach. Your hard work and commitment relieved so much stress and cognitive load, which meant I could devote more energy to making this book the best it could be. Heather Voll-trauer, thanks for keeping everything in our home running smoothly!

Heartfelt gratitude goes to my Insider's Team, who read early drafts and provided invaluable feedback. Not only did your stories influence the direction of this book, but your ongoing input significantly shaped the final product. I appreciate each and every one of you.

And finally, to my clients, past and present, for the honor of serving as your coach. I am continually amazed that I get to work with such smart, caring, and driven professionals. It's a privilege to be a part of your journey. Your trust and dedication make my work incredibly rewarding.

NOTES

Introduction

3   **the number of professionals:** This statistic comes from a study conducted by Workplace Intelligence and Oracle in 2021. Data was gathered from 14,639 full-time employees, managers, HR leaders, and C-level executives ranging in ages from twenty-two to seventy-four across thirteen countries between July 27 and August 17, 2021. To download the report, go to https://www.oracle.com/a/ocom/docs/h3hr-nurture-report.pdf.

3   **I surveyed a diverse group of twelve thousand people:** This survey was conducted from my email list and social media following beginning on July 6, 2022. The survey consisted of six open-ended questions, including *What is your definition of managing up?* and *What is your biggest struggle with managing up?*

Chapter One: The Alignment Conversation

19   **Research from Harvard Business School finds:** K. Huang et al., "It Doesn't Hurt to Ask: Question-Asking Increases Liking," *Journal of Personality and Social Psychology* 113, no. 3 (2017): 430–52, https://psycnet.apa.org/doi/10.1037/pspi0000097.

21   **caused him to feel attacked:** J. T. Dillon, *Teaching and the Art of*

Questioning (Bloomington, IN: Phi Delta Kappa Educational Foundation, 1983), 35.

21 **Another strategy I often recommend:** To learn more about Chris Voss's negotiation techniques, see his book *Never Split the Difference: Negotiating as If Your Life Depended on It* (New York: HarperCollins, 2016).

22 **this type of active listening:** Harry Weger et al., "The Relative Effectiveness of Active Listening in Initial Interactions," *International Journal of Listening* 28, no. 1 (2014): 13–31, https://doi.org/10.1080 /10904018.2013.813234.

30 **Asking questions in conversation:** Sarah Wilding et al., "The Question-Behaviour Effect: A Theoretical and Methodological Review and Meta-analysis," *European Review of Social Psychology* 27, no. 1 (2016): 196–230, https://www.tandfonline.com/doi/full/10.1080/10463283.2016.1245940.

Chapter Two: The Styles Conversation

39 **two primary dimensions shape:** Mehrdad Sarhadi, "Comparing Communication Style Within Project Teams of Three Project-Oriented Organizations in Iran," *Procedia—Social and Behavioral Sciences* 226 (2016): 226–35, https://doi.org/10.1016/j.sbspro.2016.06.183.

53 **The human brain:** Maxime Taquet et al., "Hedonism and the Choice of Everyday Activities," *PNAS* 113, no. 35 (2016): 9769–73, https://www .pnas.org/doi/pdf/10.1073/pnas.1519998113.

58 **Though it may feel nerve-racking:** Nicole You Jeung Kim et al., "You Must Have a Preference: The Impact of No-Preference Communication on Joint Decision Making," *Journal of Marketing Research* 60, no. 1 (2023): 52–71, https://doi.org/10.1177/00222437221107593.

59 **According to social exchange theory:** D. Davlembayeva and E. Alamanos, "Social Exchange Theory: A Review," in *TheoryHub Book,* ed. S. Papagiannidis, available at https://open.ncl.ac.uk/theoryhub-book/.

61 **Matching your boss's style:** R. M. Miller, K. Sanchez, and L. D. Rosenblum, "Alignment to Visual Speech Information," *Attention, Perception, & Psychophysics* 72 (2010): 1614–25, https://doi.org/10.3758 /APP.72.6.1614.

62 **activating the rewards area:** S. Kühn et al., "Why Do I Like You When You Behave Like Me? Neural Mechanisms Mediating Positive Consequences of Observing Someone Being Imitated," *Social Neuroscience* 5, no. 4 (2010): 384–92, https://doi.org/10.1080/17470911003633750.

64 **Today when roughly half:** Leeron Hoory, "The State of Workplace

Communication in 2024," Forbes Advisor, March 8, 2023, https://www
.forbes.com/advisor/business/digital-communication-workplace/.

64 **make up "digital body language":** To learn more about digital body
language, see Erica Dhawan, *Digital Body Language: How to Build Trust &
Connection, No Matter the Distance* (New York: St. Martin's Press, 2021).

68 **diverse teams are actually more innovative:** Katherine W. Phillips, Katie A.
Liljenquist, and Margaret A. Neale, "Is the Pain Worth the Gain? The
Advantages and Liabilities of Agreeing with Socially Distinct Newcomers,"
Personality and Social Psychology Bulletin 35, no. 3 (2009): 336–50, https://
doi.org/10.1177/0146167208328062.

Chapter Three: The Ownership Conversation

73 ***Future of Jobs Report:*** World Economic Forum, *Future of Jobs Report 2023,*
May 2023, https://www3.weforum.org/docs/WEF_Future_of_Jobs
_2023.pdf.

73 **When you operate:** B. D. Steindórsdóttir, C. G. L. Nerstad, and K. Þ.
Magnúsdóttir, "What Makes Employees Stay? Mastery Climate,
Psychological Need Satisfaction and On-the-Job Embeddedness," *Nordic
Psychology* 73, no. 1 (2021): 91–115, https://doi.org/10.1080/19012276.2020
.1817770.

76 **Pre-suasion, a term coined by:** To learn more about pre-suasion, see
Robert B. Cialdini, *Pre-Suasion: A Revolutionary Way to Influence and
Persuade* (New York: Simon & Schuster, 2016). I also recommend
Dr. Cialdini's first book, *Influence: The Psychology of Persuasion* (New York:
Harper Business, 2006).

77 **leveraging the psychological concept of priming:** Kai Sassenberg et al.,
"Priming Creativity as a Strategy to Increase Creative Performance by
Facilitating the Activation and Use of Remote Associations," *Journal of
Experimental Social Psychology* 68 (2017): 128–38, https://doi.org/10.1016
/j.jesp.2016.06.010.

79 **Start small:** Arthur L. Beaman et al., "Fifteen Years of Foot-in-the Door
Research: A Meta-analysis," *Personality and Social Psychology Bulletin* 9,
no. 2 (1983): 181–96, https://doi.org/10.1177/0146167283092002.

82 **concept of operational transparency:** Ryan Buell, "Operational
Transparency: Make Your Processes Visible to Customers and Your
Customers Visible to Employees," *Harvard Business Review* 97, no. 4
(2019): 102–13, https://www.hbs.edu/faculty/Pages/item.aspx?num=55804.

82 **Open loops make the brain:** A. de Berker et al., "Computations of

Uncertainty Mediate Acute Stress Responses in Humans," *Nature Communications* 7 (2016), https://doi.org/10.1038/ncomms10996.

83 **When Citicorp and Travelers merged:** Graphic designer Paula Scher shared the story of designing the Citi logo in a video interview posted by the design agency AbelsonTaylor on Vimeo: https://vimeo.com/291821523.

83 **The things that come easily to you:** D. Stuart Conger and Dana Mullen, "Life Skills," *International Journal for the Advancement of Counselling* 4 (1981): 305–19, https://link.springer.com/article/10.1007/BF00118327.

84 **A study by Gallup found:** Peter Flade, Jim Asplund, and Gwen Elliot, "Employees Who Use Their Strengths Outperform Those Who Don't," Gallup, October 8, 2015, https://www.gallup.com/workplace/236561 /employees-strengths-outperform-don.aspx.

84 **When the average attention span:** Alexander J. Simon et al., "Quantifying Attention Span Across the Lifespan," *Frontiers in Cognition 2* (2023), https://doi.org/10.3389/fcogn.2023.1207428.

85 **Leverage the center-stage effect:** Ana Valenzuela and Priya Raghubir, "Position-Based Beliefs: The Center-Stage Effect," *Journal of Consumer Psychology* 19, no. 2 (2009): 185–96, https://doi.org/10.1016/j.jcps.2009 .02.011.

87 **Creating space for people:** Charlan J. Nemeth and Brendan Nemeth-Brown, "Better Than Individuals? The Potential Benefits of Dissent and Diversity for Group Creativity," in *Group Creativity: Innovation Through Collaboration,* ed. Paul B. Paulus and Bernard A. Nijstad (New York: Oxford University Press, 2003), 63–84.

89 **Using appreciative inquiry:** Anne T. Coghlan, Hallie Preskill, and Tessie Tzavaras Castsambas, "An Overview of Appreciative Inquiry in Evaluation," *New Directions for Evaluation* 2003, no. 100 (2003): 5–22, https://doi.org/10.1002/ev.96.

89 **Shifting to the royal "we":** Ewa Kacewicz et al., "Pronoun Use Reflects Standings in Social Hierarchies," *Journal of Language and Social Psychology* 33, no. 2 (2014): 125–43, https://doi.org/10.1177/0261927X13502654.

Chapter Four: The Boundaries Conversation

95 **Research finds that employees:** Mark Bolino and Adam Grant, "The Bright Side of Being Prosocial at Work, and the Dark Side, Too: A Review and Agenda for Research on Other-Oriented Motives, Behavior, and Impact in Organizations," *Academy of Management Annals,* 2016, https:// faculty.wharton.upenn.edu/wp-content/uploads/2016/04/Bolino Grant_Annals2016_2.pdf.

96   **or non-promotable tasks:** Linda Babcock et al., "Gender Differences in Accepting and Receiving Requests for Tasks with Low Promotability," *American Economic Review* 107, no. 3 (2017): 714–47, https://www.aeaweb .org/articles?id=10.1257/aer.20141734.

98   **"the four feelings test":** This is an exercise that appears in my first book, *Trust Yourself: Stop Overthinking and Channel Your Emotions for Success at Work* (San Francisco: Chronicle Prism, 2021), 116–21.

102   **Turnover costs more than $1 trillion a year:** Charlotte Hampton, "Unhappy Workers Cost US Firms $1.9 Trillion," Bloomberg, January 23, 2024, https://www.bloomberg.com/news/articles/2024-01-23/unhappy-at -work-quit-quitting-costs-us-1-9-trillion-in-productivity.

Chapter Five: The Feedback Conversation

124   **In one survey:** Jack Zenger and Joe Folkman, "Feedback: The Powerful Paradox," Zenger Folkman, 2015, https://zengerfolkman.com/wp-content /uploads/2019/05/EF%E2%80%94White-Paper%E2%80%94Feedback -The-Powerful-Paradox.pdf.

127   **Most intense emotions:** Phillip Verduyn and Saskia Lavrijsen, "Which Emotions Last Longest and Why: The Role of Event Importance and Rumination," *Motivation and Emotion* 39 (2015): 119–27, https://doi .org/10.1007/s11031-014-9445-y.

131   **Getting this "micro-yes":** Mario Pandelaere et al., "Better Think Before Agreeing Twice. Mere Agreement: A Similarity-Based Persuasion Mechanism," *International Journal of Research in Marketing* 27, no. 2 (2010): 133–41, https://doi.org/10.1016/j.ijresmar.2010.01.003.

141   **Focusing on repair:** Kimberly McCarthy, "An Integrated Model of Relationship Repair: Reintroducing the Roles of Forgiveness and Trust," *Journal of Organizational Culture, Communications and Conflict* 21, no. 1 (2017), https://scholarworks.calstate.edu/downloads/sf2685799.

142   **up to 53 percent:** Kellie Wong, "5 Examples of How to Provide Employee Feedback for Managers," Achievers, May 31, 2023, https://www.achievers .com/blog/feedback-for-managers/.

142   **recognition lights up:** Keise Izuma, Daisuke N. Saito, and Norihiro Sadato, "Processing of Social and Monetary Rewards in the Human Striatum," *Neuron* 58, no. 2 (2008): 284–94, https://doi.org/10.1016/j.neuron.2008 .03.020.

142   **For the best results:** Kyle Benson, "The Magic Relationship Ratio, According to Science," Gottman Institute, https://www.gottman.com /blog/the-magic-relationship-ratio-according-science/.

Chapter Six: The Networking Conversation

150 **how you build social capital:** Taylor Lauricella et al., "Network Effects: How to Rebuild Social Capital and Improve Corporate Performance," McKinsey & Company, August 2, 2022, https://www.mckinsey.com /capabilities/people-and-organizational-performance/our-insights /network-effects-how-to-rebuild-social-capital-and-improve-corporate -performance.

151 **Thanks to the mere-exposure effect:** R. B. Zajonc, "Mere Exposure: A Gateway to the Subliminal," *Current Directions in Psychological Science* 10, no. 6 (2001): 224–28, https://doi.org/10.1111/1467-8721.00154.

154 **demonstrate that you're competent and likable:** Beatrice Biancardi, Angelo Cafaro, and Catherine Pelachaud, "Analyzing First Impressions of Warmth and Competence from Observable Nonverbal Cues in Expert-Novice Interactions," *Proceedings of the 19th Association for Computing Machinery International Conference on Multimodal Interaction* (2017): 341–49, https:// doi.org/10.1145/3136755.3136779.

157 **The average worker receives:** Matt Plummer, "How to Spend Way Less Time on Email Every Day," *Harvard Business Review*, January 22, 2019, https://hbr.org/2019/01/how-to-spend-way-less-time-on-email-every-day.

160 **you can express highly contagious *positive* emotions:** Yu Kong, "Are Emotions Contagious? A Conceptual Review of Studies in Language Education," *Frontiers in Psychology* 13 (2022), https://www.ncbi.nlm.nih .gov/pmc/articles/PMC9635851/.

164 **The more someone:** Ananya Mandal, "Researchers Find Talking About Ourselves Triggers Sensation of Pleasure," News-Medical Life Sciences, May 8, 2012, https://www.news-medical.net/news/20120508/Researchers -find-talking-about-ourselves-triggers-sensation-of-pleasure.aspx.

168 **When we're surprised:** Kristen Meinzer, "Surprise! Why the Unexpected Feels Good, and Why It's Good for Us," WNYC Studios, April 1, 2015, https://www.wnycstudios.org/podcasts/takeaway/segments/surprise -unexpected-why-it-feels-good-and-why-its-good-us.

169 **When you offer assistance:** Larry Dossey, "The Helper's High," *Explore* 14, no. 6 (2018): 393–99, https://doi.org/10.1016/j.explore.2018.10.003.

169 **Being of service also triggers reciprocity:** Bram P. Buunk and Wilmar B. Schaufeli, "Reciprocity in Interpersonal Relationships: An Evolutionary Perspective on Its Importance for Health and Well-Being," *European Review of Social Psychology* 10 (1999): 259–91, https://doi.org/10.1080/147 92779943000080.

171   **A great photo:** This statistic is cited in LinkedIn's help center article for
       "settings for profile photo visibility": https://www.linkedin.com/help
       /linkedin/answer/a545557/settings-for-profile-photo-visibility.

172   **grow your network of "weak ties":** Karthik Rajkumar et al., "A Causal Test
       of the Strength of Weak Ties," *Science* 377, no. 6612 (2022): 1304–10,
       https://www.science.org/doi/10.1126/science.abl4476.

Chapter Seven: The Visibility Conversation

179   **This taps into the availability heuristic:** Norbert Schwarz et al., "Ease of
       Retrieval as Information: Another Look at the Availability Heuristic,"
       Social Science Open Access Repository, 1990, https://www.ssoar.info
       /ssoar/handle/document/6723.

179   **bring visibility to your promotable work:** Linda Babcock et al., "Are You
       Taking on Too Many Non-Promotable Tasks?," *Harvard Business Review,*
       April 26, 2022, https://hbr.org/2022/04/are-you-taking-on-too-many
       -non-promotable-tasks.

182   **Listeners are twenty-two times more likely:** Jennifer Aaker, behavioral
       scientist and professor at Stanford, discusses this finding in a video for
       Stanford's VMware Women's Leadership Innovation Lab: https://womens
       leadership.stanford.edu/node/796/harnessing-power-stories.

182   **known as neural coupling:** Greg J. Stephens, Lauren J. Silbert, and Uri
       Hasson, "Speaker–Listener Neural Coupling Underlies Successful
       Communication," *PNAS* 107, no. 32 (2010): 14425–30, https://doi.org/10
       .1073/pnas.1008662107.

184   **subtly pull in social proof:** Tina A. G. Venema et al., "When in Doubt,
       Follow the Crowd? Responsiveness to Social Proof Nudges in the Absence
       of Clear Preferences," *Frontiers in Psychology* 11 (2020), https://doi.org
       /10.3389/fpsyg.2020.01385.

184   **your body releases endorphins:** Dariush Dfarhud, Maryam Malmir, and
       Mohammad Khanahmadi, "Happiness & Health: The Biological Factors–
       Systematic Review Article," *Iranian Journal of Public Health* 43, no. 11
       (2014): 1468–77, https://www.ncbi.nlm.nih.gov/pmc/articles/PMC
       4449495/.

184   **activity in your brain's fear center:** R. Alexander et al., "The Neuroscience
       of Positive Emotions and Affect: Implications for Cultivating Happiness
       and Wellbeing," *Neuroscience and Biobehavioral Reviews* 121 (2021):
       220–49, https://doi.org/10.1016/j.neubiorev.2020.12.002.

186   **thanks to the halo effect:** Tracey S. Dagger et al., "Selective Halo Effects

Arising from Improving the Interpersonal Skills of Frontline Employees," *Journal of Service Research* 16, no. 4 (2013): 488–502, https://doi.org/10 .1177/1094670513481406.

192　**can enhance your status:** Mona Weiss, "Speaking Up and Moving Up: How Voice Can Enhance Employees' Social Status," *Journal of Organizational Behavior* 40, no. 4 (2017), https://www.researchgate.net /publication/321832899_Speaking_Up_and_Moving_Up_How_Voice _Can_Enhance_Employees%27_Social_Status.

192　**making sure your contributions are timely:** Michael R. Parke et al., "How Strategic Silence Enables Employee Voice to Be Valued and Rewarded," *Organizational Behavior and Human Decision Processes* 173 (2022), https:// doi.org/10.1016/j.obhdp.2022.104187.

192　**According to the primacy effect:** Patrick Van Erkel and Peter Thijssen, "The First One Wins: Distilling the Primacy Effect," *Electoral Studies* 44 (2016): 245–54, https://doi.org/10.1016/j.electstud.2016.09.002.

192　**before your fear response:** Fuschia M. Sirois and Timothy A. Pychyl, "Procrastination and the Priority of Short-Term Mood Regulation: Consequences for Future Self," *Social and Personality Psychology Compass* 7, no. 2 (2013): 115–27, https://doi.org/10.1111/spc3.12011.

193　**Dr. Lois Frankel:** Dr. Frankel shared this quote with me in an interview for *Forbes* published on July 14, 2020. I'd recommend reading her book *Nice Girls Don't Get the Corner Office: Unconscious Mistakes Women Make That Sabotage Their Careers* (New York: Business Plus, 2014).

194　**"out of sight, out of mind":** Ward van Zoonen, Anu E. Sivunen, and Kirsimarja Blomqvist, "Out of Sight—Out of Trust? An Analysis of the Mediating Role of Communication Frequency and Quality in the Relationship Between Workplace Isolation and Trust," *European Management Journal* (2023), https://doi.org/10.1016/j.emj.2023.04.006.

Chapter Eight: The Advancement Conversation

213　**will raise your chances:** Jasmijn C. Bol, Justin Leiby, and Margaret B. Shackell, "Are You Promotable?," *Strategic Finance,* July 1, 2022, https:// www.sfmagazine.com/articles/2022/july/are-you-promotable/.

226　**Humans are innately loss averse:** K. Ruggeri et al., "Replicating Patterns of Prospect Theory for Decision Under Risk," *Nature Human Behavior* 4 (2020): 622–33, https://doi.org/10.1038/s41562-020-0886-x.

229　**known as job crafting:** Amy Wrzesniewski and Jane E. Dutton, "Crafting a Job: Revisioning Employees as Active Crafters of Their Work," *Academy of*

Management Review 26, no. 2 (2001), https://doi.org/10.5465/amr.2001
.4378011.

Chapter Nine: The Money Conversation

234   **miss out on as much:** Jenna Goudreau, "Not Negotiating Your Salary Could
       Cost $1 Million over Time," *Business Insider*, September 23, 2013, https://
       www.businessinsider.com/not-negotiating-costs-workers-1-million-2013-9.

236   **perceived as "less nice":** Mary Wade, "Women and Salary Negotiation: The
       Costs of Self-Advocacy," *Psychology of Women Quarterly* (2003), https://doi
       .org/10.1111/1471-6402.00008.

236   **more "difficult" and "demanding":** Morela Hernandez et al., "Bargaining
       While Black: The Role of Race in Salary Negotiations," *Journal of Applied
       Psychology* 104, no. 4 (2019): 581–92, https://doi.org/10.1037/apl0000363.

237   **"Fuck You, Pay Me":** This phrase originally comes from the 1990 film
       Goodfellas, but I personally first came across it in Mike Monteiro's
       CreativeMornings talk in 2011, which you can watch here: https://
       creativemornings.com/talks/mike-monteiro—2/1. It struck a nerve and is
       the most popular CreativeMornings talk of all time.

242   **The national average for a raise:** This data comes from Payscale's 2024
       Compensation Best Practices Report. A summary can be found here:
       https://www.payscale.com/press-releases/payscale-2024-compensation-best
       -practices-report-press-release/.

246   **People are more likely to respond:** Nancy A. Welsh, "Perception of Fairness
       in Negotiation," *Marquette Law Review* 87, no. 4 (2004): 753–67, https://
       scholarship.law.marquette.edu/cgi/viewcontent.cgi?article=1196&context
       =mulr.

248   **Negotiators who pause:** J. R. Curhan et al., "Silence Is Golden: Extended
       Silence, Deliberative Mindset, and Value Creation in Negotiation," *Journal
       of Applied Psychology* 107, no. 1 (2022): 78–94, https://doi.org/10.1037
       /apl0000877.

251   **But the more you confront:** Hakan Fischer et al., "Brain Habituation
       During Repeated Exposure to Fearful and Neutral Faces: A Functional
       MRI Study," *Brain Research Bulletin* 59, no. 5 (2003): 387–92, https://
       pubmed.ncbi.nlm.nih.gov/12507690/.

251   **Another way to get exposure:** Uta Herbst, Hilla Dotan, and Sina Stoehr,
       "Negotiating with Work Friends: Examining Gender Differences in Team
       Negotiations," *Journal of Business & Industrial Marketing* (2017), https://www
       .emerald.com/insight/content/doi/10.1108/JBIM-12-2015-0250/full/html.

252 **brain gives 12.5 times more weight:** Vanessa Van Edwards shares this statistic in her 2017 TEDxLondon talk "You Are Contagious": https://www.youtube.com/watch?v=cef35Fk7YD8.

252 **making your statements more memorable:** Seokmin Kang and Barbara Tversky, "From Hands to Minds: Gestures Promote Understanding," *Cognitive Research: Principles and Implications* (2016), https://cognitiveresearchjournal.springeropen.com/articles/10.1186/s41235-016-0004-9.

252 **hand gestures help you remember:** Andrew Bass, "Why Do We Gesticulate?," American Association for the Advancement of Science, July 2, 2013, https://www.eurekalert.org/news-releases/746585.

252 **Van Edwards advises:** Vanessa Van Edwards, "60 Hand Gestures You Should Be Using and Their Meaning," Science of People, June 13, 2024, https://www.scienceofpeople.com/hand-gestures/.

253 **which can make you appear:** Jinni A. Harrigan, John R. Kues, and Joseph G. Weber, "Impressions of Hand Movements: Self-Touching and Gestures," *Perceptual and Motor Skills* 63, no. 2 (1986), https://journals.sagepub.com/doi/10.2466/pms.1986.63.2.503.

253 **increase feelings of self-consciousness:** Kristine M. Kuhn, "The Constant Mirror: Self-View and Attitudes to Virtual Meetings," *Computers in Human Behavior* 128 (2022), https://doi.org/10.1016/j.chb.2021.107110.

253 **Kim Scott:** Kim Scott is the author of *Radical Candor: Be a Kick-Ass Boss Without Losing Your Humanity* (New York: St. Martin's Press, 2017), but her tip to use "it" statements comes from her book *Radical Respect: How to Work Together Better* (New York: St. Martin's Press, 2024).

255 **Yes, studies show:** Amy Gallo, "Setting the Record Straight: Using an Outside Offer to Get a Raise," *Harvard Business Review,* July 5, 2016, https://hbr.org/2016/07/setting-the-record-straight-using-an-outside-offer-to-get-a-raise.

Chapter Ten: The Quitting Conversation

260 **Thanks to the peak-end effect:** Daniel Kahneman et al., "When More Pain Is Preferred to Less: Adding a Better End," *Psychological Science* 4, no. 6 (1993): 401–5, https://www.jstor.org/stable/40062570.

260 **More than 70 percent of professionals:** This data comes from a LinkedIn online survey conducted from February 6 to March 18, 2017, among 15,905 LinkedIn members across seventeen countries: https://news.linkedin.com/2017/6/eighty-percent-of-professionals-consider-networking-important-to-career-success.

261 **Nearly 30 percent of employees "boomerang":** Anthony C. Klotz et al., "The Promise (and Risk) of Boomerang Employees," *Harvard Business Review*, March 15, 2023, https://hbr.org/2023/03/the-promise-and-risk -of-boomerang-employees.

261 **pairing intuition with analytical thinking:** Galang Lufityanto, Chris Donkin, and Joel Pearson, "Measuring Intuition: Nonconscious Emotional Information Boosts Decision Accuracy and Confidence," *Psychological Science* 27, no. 5 (2016), https://doi.org/10.1177/0956797616629403.

263 **known as defensive pessimism:** Julie Norem and Nancy Cantor, "Defensive Pessimism: Harnessing Anxiety as Motivation," *Journal of Personality and Social Psychology* 51, no. 6 (1986): 1208–17, https://doi.org/10.1037//0022 -3514.51.6.1208.

263 **feel more comfortable with your choice:** Paola Magnano, Anna Paolillo, and Barbara Giacominelli, "Dispositional Optimism as a Correlate of Decision-Making Styles in Adolescence," *SAGE Open* (2015), https://doi .org/10.1177/2158244015592002.

270 **quitting contagion:** Will Felps et al., "Turnover Contagion: How Coworkers' Job Embeddedness and Job Search Behaviors Influence Quitting," *Academy of Management Journal* 52, no. 3 (2017), https://journals .aom.org/doi/abs/10.5465/amj.2009.41331075.

275 **natural desire for cognitive closure:** Maria Konnikova, "Why We Need Answers," *New Yorker*, April 30, 2013, https://www.newyorker.com/tech /annals-of-technology/why-we-need-answers.

INDEX

About the Author

MELODY WILDING, LMSW, is an award-winning executive coach, keynote speaker, and author of *Trust Yourself: Stop Overthinking and Channel Your Emotions for Success at Work*. Named one of Insider's "most innovative career coaches," her clients include CEOs, C-level executives, and managers at top Fortune 500 companies such as Google, Amazon, Walmart, and JPMorgan-Chase, among others. A human behavior professor at Hunter College in New York City, Melody uses her background as a therapist and emotions researcher to inform her unique approach—weaving evidence-based neuroscience and psychology with career and professional development.

Her work has been featured in *The New York Times, The Wall Street Journal,* and dozens of other national media outlets. She is a contributor to *Harvard Business Review, Fast Company, Psychology Today,* and *Forbes*. Melody is a licensed social worker with a master's degree from Columbia University. She lives in New Jersey with her husband, Brian. Learn more about her programs and speaking at melodywilding.com.